AND WHEN THEY BEGAN TO SING...

Understanding God's Purpose
for
the Music Ministry

AND WHEN THEY BEGAN TO SING...

Understanding God's Purpose for the Music Ministry

By
ALVIN D. FRUGA

PUBLISHING·INC

Tulsa, Oklahoma

And When They Began To Sing
(Understanding God's Purpose for the Music Ministry)
ISBN   0-9657706-0-5
Copyright © 1997 by
Alvin D. Fruga
P.O. Box 54542
Tulsa, Oklahoma 74155

Published by
PHOS Publishing Company
Tulsa, Oklahoma

Printed in the United States of America.

Dedication

This book is dedicated to
the memory of my mother

JOYCE A. FRUGA

My mom had a chance to read the first draft of this book long before she went to heaven. She was so excited that one of her children was actually writing a book. My mother always encouraged me to go after my dreams, while at the same time she taught me the importance of humility before God and man. She was anointed to touch people's lives, and she always did it with a smile. Her legacy of love, creativity, and the unwavering pursuit of fulfilling one's God-given destiny while on this earth, lives on through the lives of her four children.

Contents

Acknowledgements

I want to thank my pastor, Bishop Carlton D. Pearson, for encouraging me to step out, seize the moment, and ride the God-ordained waves of life. Your friendship and support of my ministry have been a continual blessing in my life. Thanks to the Higher Dimensions Family Church and Sanctuary Choir for allowing me to share my gifts and talents with you. We win!

To JoAnne Cramberg for not only believing in the message of this book, but more importantly for believing in the author. Thank you for helping me to make this happen, and for going the extra mile to ensure that we put out a fresh project.

Special thanks to my three siblings and their spouses: my sister, Jeanice Williams and her husband Jack, my elder brother, Willie Fruga Jr. and his wife, Sandra, and my younger, but taller, brother, DeJon Fruga and his wife Christina. Your constant love and prayer support have been a tremendous blessing to Sennola and me. We love you!

To my dad, Willie Fruga Sr., who taught me how to play the piano at a young age, and inspired me into the music ministry by allowing me to hang out with him at rehearsals and church services. Thanks, Dad!

Love and honor to my childhood sweetheart and best friend, my beautiful wife, Sennola, who never ceases to support me in all my ministry endeavors. You are truly SENNOLARRIFIC!

And to my four priceless gifts, my children, Michael, Teree, Kambri and Shannon, for always reminding me that ministry begins at home. Superdad loves you.

Foreword

Singing is a verb, an action word. In the Bible singing was much more than the first and third stanzas of a denominational hymnal on Sunday morning. To the Old Testament Jews, singing was an active part of everyday activity as well as worship.

Repeatedly throughout the Bible, we are admonished to sing on all occasions — in praise of what God has done and in anticipation of the future. We further sing in worship of God for who He is. Singing, for the Christian, is not just a command, but rather a natural outgrowth of a relationship with the Father.

The first appearance of singing in scripture is in the 15th chapter of the book of Exodus, when Moses and the Israelites sang to the Lord.

> **I will sing unto the Lord, for he hath triumphed gloriously: the horse and his rider hath he thrown into the sea. The LORD is my strength and song, and he is become my salvation: he is my God, and I will prepare him an habitation; my father's God, and I will exalt him.**

> **Exodus 15:1b-2 KJV**

The singing was a result of Israel's original exit from 400 years of Egyptian slavery and bondage. It was obviously a time of rejoicing.

Singing is typically a sign of not only worship, adoration and praise, but it reflects freedom and deliverance from the fear, bondage and tyranny of sin.

The ministry of music has been instrumental in my life and at the core of my ministry for over twenty years. I have seen the effect of music ministry in "breaking up the fallow ground" and preparing the human heart to receive an infusion of the Spirit of God.

Alvin Fruga is uniquely qualified to write about this much needed subject. The what, when, how and why of music ministry in both the Church and in the personal worship experience are powerful and very well explained.

Alvin was our minister of music at Higher Dimensions Family Church for several years, and has ministered with me throughout Europe, Africa, the North American continent and the islands of the sea. In every situation, including the recent passing of his mother, he practices what he teaches.

His anointed involvement with our last three album projects, writing many of the songs, directing, singing, and co-producing with Warner Alliance, has produced the greatest response to our ministry yet.

Recently, Alvin launched his own full-time ministry, Fresh Oil Ministries, and despite a busy travelling schedule he and his family remain active in our church and ministry.

John 4:23 says that the Father is seeking worshippers who will worship Him in spirit and truth. When you have read and applied *And When They Began To Sing* . . . you will be equipped as a true worshipper.

Bishop Carlton D. Pearson
Higher Dimensions Family Church
Tulsa, Oklahoma

Introduction

"Daddy, can I go with you to choir rehearsal tonight?" I can remember asking my father this question every week, during most of my childhood. As a young boy fascinated by music, I loved going to choir rehearsal with my dad. Not just to hear the choir sing, although that was a part of it, but more importantly to see my dad in action. He was not just a choir member. He was the music director.

I can remember sitting on the edge of my seat in choir rehearsals and church services watching my dad teach, direct, and motivate both singers and musicians to the point where they would give absolutely everything they had musically and spiritually in praise to the Lord. Of course I said, as most boys do, "I want to be just like my dad." It was amazing to me how he could, with seemingly little effort, teach all the choir parts, from first soprano to bass. My Dad is also an accomplished musician. He knew exactly what each band member was supposed to play, and when. He had such a confident command of everything that was taking place musically within a church service. Yes, I definitely wanted to be a chip off the old block.

No wonder it was such an easy transition for me, when I became a teenager, to go from being on the sidelines to actually singing in the church choir. I still remember the awesome feeling of standing in front of the congregation for the first time as a choir member. I would never be the same. The many things I learned musically, and the friendships I developed, are experiences that I will never forget. I can even remember singing in my first choir concert. Black pants, white shirt, black tie, and eyes bugged out wide with uncontrollable excitement. I had to stand in the front row of the tenor section because I was so short. I've grown a little since then, and I no longer have the black pants, shirt or tie. But I still haven't figured out how to control my eyes.

I have fond memories of long choir trips to other churches. We would sing an entire concert for the bus driver before we ever arrived at our destination. I remember going to choir fellowships at a member's home. We would have a great time eating, laughing at things that happened in church, eating again, playing games...eating, and of course, singing. We always sang. It wasn't long before I was directing choirs myself. I was doing exactly what I had observed my father do for years. As a musician, I spent countless hours teaching, directing, and yes, even motivating singers and musicians. I eventually realized that music ministry was my calling, and I would be involved in this area of ministry the rest of my life. This revelation of my call, along with the desire to give God my very best, caused me to ask some very important questions. How did the music ministry originate? And why? What is the purpose for music in the church?

All right, I'll be real honest with you. After being a choir member for years, and subsequently a music director, I realized I didn't really know the spiritual reasons for what I was doing. Oh yes, I knew I was giving glory to God, and I knew He had called me to the music ministry. But I honestly did not know God's original intent and purpose for music in the church. All I knew was that music helped to make the service flow better, providing a sort of Christian entertainment for the congregation.

Now, you be honest with me, and yourself. Do you know God's purpose for music in the church? Do you have a clear understanding of what was in His heart when He first instituted this ministry? I submit to you that the music ministry serves a much more meaningful purpose than simply filling space in a service, or providing some type of entertainment for the congregation. There is a specific spiritual role that music plays in a service, which can be traced back to its origin in scripture.

The Lord has shared with me some exciting truths regarding the music ministry. It has totally revolutionized my thinking, and sharpened my spiritual focus during church services. I thank God that I now not only know what I'm doing, I know why I'm doing it. It is for this reason that I have written this book. I have a deep concern for pastors, music directors, choir members, and congregational members who may not fully understand the purpose for the music ministry. Many of us understand the musical aspects, but not the spiritual aspects. What spiritual purpose does music serve in the church? What actually takes place in the spirit realm when we sing praises to God? Why does the enemy try so hard to come against the infrastructure of our music programs, doing all he can to create division and disunity? Why is the music ministry such a threat to him? If we do not know the answers to these questions, we can never be totally effective in our call.

Music plays a vital role within a church service. Although nothing can take the place of the spoken Word of God, the music ministry is very significant, because it prepares the congregation to receive the Word. The singing of a choir accompanied by musicians can easily be compared to the ministry of John the Baptist, in that it is the voice of one crying in the wilderness, "Prepare ye the way of the Lord" (Luke 3:4). A choir singing in unity is one voice crying out in worship to the Lord.

Their mission is to prepare, repair, recondition, and purify the spiritual atmosphere in order for the Word to fall on good ground. Music sets the atmosphere, and paves the way for the congregation to receive the Word, and ultimately be set free. It is not the pastor's responsibility to do this. The "path" should already be clear when he or she gets up to speak. The pastor should be totally free to minister the Word, and the congregation ready to receive the Word, without any hindrances or distractions. This is the reason for Satan's many attacks. He knows that if the congregation receives the truth, they will live more victoriously.

It is my desire to expose this deception of the enemy, and reveal and release God's truth concerning the music ministry, so we can begin to experience some of the same results as the children of Israel "when they began to sing." Whether you are a pastor, music director, musician, choir member, or parishioner, my prayer is that through this book you will gain a fresh and renewed understanding of God's purpose for the music ministry, and that you will take the necessary steps to insure that the music program in your church is fulfilling its purpose.

It's been almost twenty-five years since the time when I asked my dad to go to choir rehearsals with him. I can still hear those words loud and clear, "Daddy, can I go with you to choir rehearsal tonight?" Only now, it's my children asking me.

1
Biblical History of the Music Ministry

The first step to gaining a better understanding of God's purpose for the music ministry is to take a look back into biblical history and see how, when and why it originated. This will give us invaluable insight as to what the purpose of our music programs should be today. As you embark on this exciting musical journey into God's Word, He will unveil some of the most wonderful truths regarding the music ministry that you have ever known.

Moses' Era

The history of music in the temple first dates back to Moses' day between 1300 and 1200 BC. It centers around the care of, and worship in the Tent of Meeting, the place where the Israelites often met with God. The very foundation and purpose for music in the Church was definitely established during this period.

In Exodus chapter 32, Moses is on Mt. Sinai receiving the law and commandments of the Lord written on tablets of stone. He had been up there continually since chapter 24, which covered a period of forty days and forty nights (Exodus 24:18). The children of Israel had just entered into a covenant with God to worship and obey Him only. However, the children of Israel became

1

impatient with Moses and the "God" Who was speaking to him on the mountain. So with the help of Aaron they made their own god from their gold earrings. They melted down the earrings, and fashioned them into the form of a golden calf. They sacrificed burnt offerings to this god, and worshipped it with singing and dancing. As a result of the Israelites' corruption, God sent Moses down from Mt. Sinai to deal with Israel's sinful acts.

> **And the Lord said unto Moses, Go, get thee down; for thy people, which thou broughtest out of the land of Egypt, have corrupted themselves.**
>
> **Exodus 32:7 KJV**

Notice here that God is already disturbed with the children of Israel by the way He refers to them. He now addresses them as Moses' people, whom Moses brought out of Egypt, rather than His people whom He brought out of Egypt. In fact, if it hadn't been for Moses pleading the Israelites' case, God would have totally destroyed them all (vv. 9-14). What a great example of God's mercy toward His people. Although He chastised them, He did not utterly destroy them.

As Moses and Joshua came down from the mountain they heard a noise which Joshua described as a sound of war. However, Moses disagreed with this description. This was not a sound of war, because the noise was not a cry of defeat, nor was it a cry of victory (vv. 15-18). Moses described it as "the noise of them that sing." It was apparently a familiar sound to Moses, because he was able to distinguish what kind of noise it was. There is not much information given to us concerning Moses' childhood, except the fact that he was born a Hebrew, and raised an Egyptian. However, one could suggest, from Exodus 2:11, that Moses often went to where his own people were to watch them work, and maybe even hear them sing. Yes, this was definitely a sound Moses had heard many times before.

Unfortunately, this particular singing by the Israelites was to the wrong god. In just forty-two days the Israelites had already broken their covenant with God, and once again committed idolatry. As Moses reached the edge of the camp, he saw firsthand the idolatry of God's people, and became very angry. He broke the tablets of stone as an outward sign of Israel's broken covenant with God (v. 19). He also burned the golden calf, ground it into powder, mixed it with water, and made the Israelites drink it (v. 20). But that wasn't all Moses did. After giving Aaron a stiff talking to, Moses realized the people were naked and had shamed themselves before their enemies. It was at this time that Moses asked one of the most important and pivotal questions in the history of all mankind.

> **Who is on the Lord's side? let him come unto me.**
>
> **Exodus 32:26 KJV**

Of all the twelve tribes of Israel, there was only one tribe who responded positively to Moses' question. Without hesitation, the Levites came to where Moses was. I'm sure this pleased Moses, because he was from the tribe of Levi. Of more significance, however, is the fact that it pleased God. Of all the twelve tribes of Israel, the Levites were the only tribe to realize their mistakes, and return to the Lord. This response by the Levites so moved God's heart that He chose them to be the only tribe to work and minister in the temple of the Lord. They would perform these duties on behalf of all of Israel.

> The Lord said to Moses, "Bring the tribe of Levi
> and present them to Aaron the priest to assist him.
> They are to perform duties for him and for the whole
> community at the Tent of Meeting by doing the work
> of the tabernacle. They are to take care of all the
> furnishings of the Tent of Meeting, fulfilling the
> obligations of the Israelites by doing the work of the
> tabernacle. Give the Levites to Aaron and his sons;
> they are the Israelites who are to be given wholly to
> him. Appoint Aaron and his sons to serve as priests;
> anyone else who approaches the sanctuary must be
> put to death."
>
> Numbers 3:5-10

God didn't stop there. He wanted all Israel to know
that the Levites were now His. So He replaced all the
firstborn males of Israel, which He had previously set
aside for Himself, with the tribe of Levi.

> The Lord also said to Moses, "I have taken the
> Levites from among the Israelites in place of the first
> male offspring of every Israelite woman. The Levites
> are mine, for all the firstborn are mine. When I struck
> down all the firstborn in Egypt, I set apart for myself
> every firstborn in Israel, whether man or animal.
> They are to be mine. I am the Lord."
>
> Numbers 3:11-13

By doing this, God established the Levites as His
eternal firstborn. The Levites were a constant reminder
to God that if no other tribe worshipped Him, they
would. They became God's personal praise remnant.
God would not allow anyone but the Levites to minister in or around the place where He dwelt.

The Levites were set aside for the express purpose
of caring for the sanctuary, and ministering before the
Lord. Their initial duties included transporting the tabernacle and its furniture whenever the camp was

moved. This included the ark of the covenant, which represented the very presence of God among the Israelites. They would also set up the Tent of Meeting, and thoroughly clean and care for it day and night. The Levites also assisted the priests who were under Aaron's leadership at that time. Other duties included doorkeeper, temple musician, and administrator.

God wanted to make it very clear that the Levites were to be *His* chosen ones to care for and minister in the Tent of Meeting. In order to accomplish this, He set them apart from the rest of the Israelites.

> **The Lord said to Moses: "Take the Levites from among the other Israelites and make them ceremonially clean."**
>
> **Numbers 8:5,6**

God wanted them separate from the rest of the tribes of Israel. He even wanted them cleaner than the rest of the tribes of Israel. He took them through a special purification process. From now on there would be distinct differences between the Levites and the rest of the tribes. Only the Levites, along with Aaron and his sons, would offer atonement for sin, thus serving as an Old Testament advocate on behalf of all Israel. The Levites were so special to God that He gave them as a gift to Aaron the priest for this specific purpose.

> **Of all the Israelites, I have given the Levites as gifts to Aaron and his sons to do the work at the Tent of Meeting on behalf of the Israelites and to make atonement for them so that no plague will strike the Israelites when they go near the sanctuary.**
>
> **Numbers 8:19**

He also gave them as a gift to ensure that the temple was properly and constantly cared for.

> **I myself have selected your fellow Levites from among the Israelites as a gift to you, dedicated to the Lord to do the work at the Tent of Meeting.**
>
> **Numbers 18:6**

I really like the use of the word *gift* in these passages, because it demonstrates God's love and concern for His Church, and the priest or pastor who has given his life to oversee the temple. God saw that Aaron needed help in the house of the Lord, so He gave him a gift. This gift came in the form of tent custodians, gatekeepers, administrators, and yes, musicians and singers. The music ministry is a gift from God to pastors and their churches, in order to assist them in the work of the ministry.

God also provided a source of payment for those who worked in the temple. The Levites would not be given an inheritance like the other tribes of Israel. They would instead receive the tithe from the other eleven tribes of Israel as their inheritance.

> **"I give to the Levites all the tithes in Israel as their inheritance in return for the work they do while serving at the Tent of Meeting. From now on the Israelites must not go near the Tent of Meeting, or they will bear the consequences of their sin and will die. It is the Levites who are to do the work at the Tent of Meeting and bear the responsibility for offenses against it. This is a lasting ordinance for the generations to come. They will receive no inheritance among the Israelites. Instead, I give to the Levites as their inheritance the tithes that the Israelites present as an offering to the Lord. That is why I said concerning them: 'They will have no inheritance among the Israelites.'"**
>
> **Numbers 18:21-24**

This gives more than adequate biblical support for paying workers in the church today, which includes musicians and singers. Most churches today at least pay their music director and musicians. But one might suggest that a church would go bankrupt if it also paid every choir member. I strongly disagree. Most churches simply suffer from improper giving habits. For example, in most churches today, only about 20 percent of the congregation supports 80 percent of the entire church budget. In other words, 80 percent of most congregations only give enough to cover 20 percent of the church expenses. As a result, we are not in the financial position to bless every person who gives their time in service to the Lord. Most choir members never think about getting paid, and might even take offense to being offered payment for something they love to do. And the ones who demand payment for their services need to recheck their motives. However, the point I'm making here is most churches today have missed the perfect plan of God as it relates to His provision for all temple workers.

In many cases, we have totally dismissed the idea of actually paying choir members on the grounds that it is financially unfeasible, when in fact, we have failed to properly teach our congregations God's all-inclusive purpose for the tithe. For the Levites, their ministry in the temple was their livelihood. They didn't have a job outside their work in the temple.

> **And these are the singers, chief of the fathers of the Levites, who remaining in the chambers were free: for they were employed in that work day and night.**
>
> **1 Chronicles 9:33 KJV**

There was no question as to what God wanted and

required. All of Israel would tithe, and that tithe would go to all those who worked in the temple. Giving the tithe was not an option, it was a command. The question is, has God changed His commands? I don't think so. What we must do is allow the truth of God's Word concerning tithing to set us free from the lies which Satan has seemingly tricked us with. When all of God's people learn the importance of tithing, and begin to financially operate solely based on His truth, the entire Body of Christ, including the area of music, will experience a mighty move of God.

When Moses asked, "Who is on the Lord's side?" the Levites realized their error, repented of worshipping the golden image, and returned to the Lord. As a result, God chose them to be the only ones who could minister to Him in the Temple of Meeting. This marks the beginning for what we know today as music ministry within the church. We can learn a lot from the Levites. They were by no means perfect. The only thing that separated them from the other host of idolaters was that they realized their mistakes, and returned to the Lord. True servants of God are those who, no matter what mistakes they make, will always find their way back to the bosom of the Father.

King David's Era

It wasn't until about 1000 BC, during the period of the kings of Israel, that a more distinct role of music in the temple is seen. The first choirs actually mentioned in the Bible appear during the reign of King David. This is not at all surprising since David was an accomplished musician, singer and songwriter from his youth. My favorite account of David was when he played the harp for King Saul. Not only was King Saul refreshed, but an evil spirit left him as a result of David's ministry (1 Samuel 16:23). This alone is evidence enough to prove that God desires for music to minister healing and deliverance to those in need.

When David became king, one of the first things he did was return the Ark of the Lord to its proper place in Jerusalem. The Ark of Covenant represented the very presence of God among the children of Israel. It was the only article of furniture, within the Temple of Meeting, which was placed in the Holy of Holies. Only the high priest could enter this innermost room of the temple once a year to offer atonement of sin for all Israel.

The ark had a gold cover which was called the mercy seat. The Israelites believed that this was the very throne of God. The ark was so sacred that whenever the Israelites moved their camp to a new location, the Levites, by God's order, were the only ones who could carry the ark. The presence of the ark among the Israelites was also a sign to them of God's approval and provision.

The ark was not always in the Israelites' camp. The Israelites were at one time defeated by the Philistines, who captured the ark from them (1 Samuel 4:1-11). However, disaster hit the camp of the Philistines due to their mishandling of the ark. It wasn't long before the Philistines sent it back (1 Samuel 5 and 6). The ark ended up in a place called Kiriath Jearim.

> So the men of Kiriath Jearim came and took up the ark of the Lord. They took it to Abinadab's house on the hill and consecrated Eleazar his son to guard the ark of the Lord. It was a long time, twenty years in all, that the ark remained at Kiriath Jearim, and all

the people of Israel mourned and sought after the
Lord.

1 Samuel 7:1,2

During this twenty-year period, which covered the
reign of King Saul, and the exile of David the future
king, the children of Israel were without the ark in
Jerusalem, and thus felt like they did not have God's
presence or approval among them. But when David
became king, he immediately took action to bring the
ark to its rightful place.

David conferred with each of his officers, the
commanders of thousands and commanders of
hundreds. He then said to the whole assembly of
Israel, "If it seems good to you and if it is the will of
the Lord our God, let us send word far and wide to
the rest of our brothers throughout the territories of
Israel, and also the priests and Levites who are with
them in their towns and pasturelands, to come and
join us. Let us bring the ark of our God back to us,
for we did not inquire of it during the reign of Saul."
The whole assembly agreed to do this, because it
seemed right to all the people.

1 Chronicles 13:1-4

David specifically asked for the priests and Levites
from the various surrounding regions of Israel to come
and join in the celebration of bringing the ark back to
Jerusalem. But for some reason he allowed Abinadab's
sons Uzzah and Ahio to guide the cart which carried
the ark. David made two costly mistakes by allowing
this to happen. First, the ark should not have been placed
on a cart. Remember, God specifically chose the Levites
to carry the ark. The Levites were to carry it on their
shoulders using the poles that slid underneath the base

of the ark, making sure never to actually touch it. This was one of their prescribed duties.

Secondly, Uzzah and Ahio were not Levites. They were from the tribe of Judah. Only the Levites were to be in close proximity to the ark. In addition to these mistakes, Uzzah committed a deadly error. He reached out and touched the ark in order to steady it. This was all that God could take. No one, not even the Levites, were to ever touch the ark. God struck Uzzah dead and stopped the procession.

The singing stopped. The music stopped. The dancing stopped.There comes a time in our praise and worship, and choir singing, when various aspects of our celebration are critically wrong. It is at these times that we must be willing to stop the music until things are corrected. We will discuss this further in chapter 5.

The reason many of our music programs lack the anointing, and sometimes even suffer spiritual defeat is because the wrong people are handling the ark. As stated before, Ahio and Uzzah were from the tribe of Judah, which translated in Hebrew means praise.[1] However, as proven by Uzzah, it's not good enough for singers and musicians to have only a spirit of praise (Judah). They must be of the tribe and spirit of Levi. The name *Levi* as translated in Hebrew means to be attached, to twine, to unite, to remain, to join or be joined.[2] This suggests that even in times of great temptation and distress, the true Levites will always return or join themselves to God. There is a divine connection between God and that Levitical spirit. Anybody can praise God, but only the Levites can handle or carry the anointing.

As a result of King David's error, and Uzzah's death, the ark did not make it to Jerusalem. It ended up at Obed-Edom's house for three months (1 Chronicles 13:12-14). King David, realizing his costly mistakes, decided to try once again to bring the ark back to Jerusalem. Only this time he would do it the way God had originally instructed. In 1 Chronicles 15 we read that David assembled the Levites and gave them specific instructions.

> He said to them, "You are the heads of the Levitical families; you and your fellow Levites are to consecrate yourselves and bring up the ark of the Lord, the God of Israel, to the place I have prepared for it. It was because you, the Levites, did not bring it up the first time that the Lord our God broke out in anger against us. We did not inquire of him about how to do it in the prescribed way."
>
> **1 Chronicles 15:12,13**

The last sentence in verse 13 is powerful! We can save ourselves a lot of unnecessary trouble and distress by taking the time to seek the Lord as to how we should bring His presence into the temple. The Levites first consecrated themselves "in order to bring up the ark of the Lord" (v. 14). Then they carried the ark with the poles on their shoulders. In other words, *after* the Levites consecrated themselves, they were free to allow the anointing to rest on them. Selah!

In verse 16 of this same chapter we see the first organized choir and orchestra, along with a minister of music. David wanted to make sure there would be singing and rejoicing taking place while the ark was being carried. So he appointed specific singers and musicians from among the Levites to perform these duties.

> David told the leaders of the Levites to appoint their brothers as singers to sing joyful songs,

accompanied by musical instruments: lyres, harps and cymbals.

1 Chronicles 15:16

This is the first biblical account of an organized music ministry. All of the musicians and singers were Levites. The rest of this chapter describes exactly who performed what duties. According to Genesis 46:11, and also 1 Chronicles 6:1, Levi, the father of the Levites, had three sons. Their names are Gershon, Kohath and Merari. In 1 Chronicles 6:31-46, a description is given as to who from these three sons of Levi were actually leaders involved in the ministry of music. From the descendants of Levi's middle son Kohath, Heman was taken. From the descendants of Levi's oldest son Gershon, Asaph was taken. And from the descendants of Levi's youngest son Merari, Ethan was chosen.

Taking this into account, we can better understand the family roots of the Levites mentioned in 1 Chronicles 15:17 and following. The following Tribe of Levi Flow Chart shows Levi's three sons and their descendants, from which came the head musicians and singers.

TRIBE OF LEVI FLOW CHART

GOD'S ORIGINAL SINGERS AND MUSICIANS

The Twelve Tribes of Israel

The Tribe of Levi

Levi's Three Sons

Gershon	Kohath	Merari
14 Generations	21 Generations	13 Generations
Asaph	Heman	Ethan

Choir Members and Musicians

Heman, Asaph, and Ethan were all musicians according to 1 Chronicles 15:19. Although they were cymbal players, they were also leaders among the musicians. It is Chenaniah (also Kenaniah), mentioned in verse 22, who was in charge of the singing. The reason he was put in charge of the singing, according to this scripture, was because "he was skillful at it." Chenaniah, who appears to have come from the Gershonites, was the choir director. He had the ability to teach all the singing, and make sure they were prepared to sing whenever King David summoned them. Bringing the ark back to Jerusalem was only the first of many times David would call for the choir.

With the musicians and singers in place, verse 25 states that David with all the commanders, leaders, musicians and singers brought the ark from the house of Obed-Edom with rejoicing. Verses 27 and 28 further describe this joyous celebration:

> Now David was clothed in a robe of fine linen, as were all the Levites who were carrying the ark, and as were the singers, and Kenaniah, who was in charge of the singing of the choirs. David also wore a linen ephod. So all Israel brought up the ark of the covenant of the Lord with shouts, with the sounding of rams' horns and trumpets, and of cymbals, and the playing of lyres and harps.

After the ark was returned to Jerusalem, 1 Chronicles 6:31 says, "...the ark had rest." It was at this time that David appointed musicians and singers to minister before the Lord continually (1 Chronicles 6:32). When this permanent resting place was provided by David during his reign, it was no longer necessary for the Levites to carry the ark. Their duties were changed to include assisting priests, judges and scribes, gatekeepers, and musicians, which of course included singers.

David appointed musicians and singers for the sole purpose of ministering unto the Lord continually with songs of praise and thanksgiving. The Levites were the leaders in the area of singing praises to God. They were the Israelite choir. David's only reason for establishing a music ministry was to provide a comfortable habitation for the presence of the Lord.

Today's purpose for the music ministry has not changed. We are to minister to the Lord, and sing praises to Him for His pleasure, and for His glory, always being aware of His presence among us. We must never get away from this central focus.

David had such an impact on temple worship that succeeding kings modeled their worship after the order David had established. When Hezekiah became king he stationed the temple musicians "...in the way prescribed by David" (2 Chronicles 29:25). The young King Josiah also made sure temple worship took place as commanded by David (2 Chronicles 35:15). Nehemiah, some 500 years after David's reign, made sure the choir ministered "according to the commandment of David the man of God" Nehemiah 12:24 KJV). It is no wonder God described David as a "man after his own heart" (1 Samuel 13:14).

King David took great care and detail in making sure the praises of God went up continually before the Lord. No king before or after him could boast of such music ministry organization with the express purpose of giving glory to God. Even when David was old and ready to pass the kingly torch to his son Solomon, he made sure that proper temple worship would take place long after he was gone. David gave specific instructions as to what the Levites' duties would be under Solomon's leadership. Out of the twenty-four thousand Levites set aside for the work of the temple, David designated four thousand to praise the Lord with musical instruments (1 Chronicles 23:1-5). Their express duties are further described in verses 30 through 32, which include singing before the Lord morning and night, as well as for special festivals and feasts:

> **They were also to stand every morning to thank and praise the Lord. They were to do the same in the evening and whenever burnt offerings were presented to the Lord on Sabbaths and at New Moon**

festivals and at appointed feasts. They were to serve before the Lord regularly in the proper number and in the way prescribed for them. And so the Levites carried out their responsibilities for the Tent of Meeting, for the Holy Place and, under their brothers the descendants of Aaron, for the service of the temple of the Lord.

1 Chronicles 23:30-32

God is always looking for those with the Levite spirit. He wants those who are willing to repent of their mistakes, and return to Him. Remember, the name *Levi* means to be attached, to join or be joined to. God knew the Levites were not mistake-proof. But He also knew that whatever they did, they would always repent and rejoin themselves to Him, and with one another in temple worship. To be effective in the choir ministry we must always be aware of the importance of adjoining or aligning ourselves with the Father, and joining or connecting ourselves with one another.

It is important to notice there was no congregation for whom the choir sang. There was never a congregation in the temple. The children of Israel would worship from the outer courts. The only ones actually in the temple were the priests and the Levites, who ministered unto the Lord. The singing of the Levites was not for the benefit of the people. It was only for the pleasure of the Father.

Although the new covenant opened the door for all to come in the temple and worship, the purpose for music and singing in the temple has not changed. The ministry of music must always be directed first to the Lord, for His glory. The congregation receives the residual benefit of the singing, but the central theme and focus should always be to minister to the Lord, and provide a habitation for His presence.

2

Requirements for Ministering in the Temple

There are certain requirements that must be met before a person can minister in the temple of the Lord. Simply having the ability to sing or play an instrument is only a fraction of what it takes to be an effective music minister. Remember, anybody can praise (Judah), but it takes those with the spirit of Levi to be effective in ministry.

God took the Levites through a process of preparation before they ever sang a note. They had to meet His requirements before He would allow them to be His special praise force. Likewise, before we can minister, we must also meet His requirements. In taking another brief look at the calling of the Levites, as it occurred in Exodus chapter 32, we see there are five requirements which must be met in order to effectively serve. They are:

1. Make a decision

2. Kill what is dear to you

3. Be thoroughly cleansed

4. Carry the burden

5. Have the ability to minister

Make a Decision

When Moses asked the question, "Who is on the Lord's side?" the Levites were the only tribe to decide to gather themselves where Moses was, thus choosing to be on the Lord's side. This is the first step to meeting God's requirements for ministry. The decision the Levites made was a life decision to follow God and all His ways. It wasn't a decision to be involved in ministry. This decision had nothing to do with working in the temple or singing in a choir. It was a decision to turn from their wicked ways and follow the Lord.

Likewise, our decision to be on the Lord's side should have nothing to do with any aspirations we may have to minister. The decision we make to surrender our lives to God is based solely on the fact that we have recognized the error of our ways and realize He is the only one who can bring about a true change in our lives. We cannot consider our salvation as a stepping-stone or a means to an end. Our decision to live for Christ is "the" single most important decision we will ever make.

With all the talent you may possess, would you still love God and wholly dedicate your life to Him if He told you never to sing or play an instrument again? Would this change your life decision? When we make a decision to be on the Lord's side, we embark on a new and exciting road toward fulfilling God's will for our lives. A portion of His will for our lives might entail being involved in the music ministry. But the overall ramifications of our decision extend far beyond what we feel called to do.

The Levites made their decision because they wanted to save their lives. They never expected God to call them to the full-time ministry. They were just glad to escape His wrath. They were just glad to be saved. It really is no different with us. At least it shouldn't be. Our decision to come to Christ should be because we realize He is the only One Who can save us from sin and death. This should be the only motivation for our decision. After we make this decision, then we should earnestly seek His guidance as to how we can best serve Him. If God calls us to the music ministry, great! But if He doesn't, that's OK. We are still saved and have escaped the inevitable wrath that is to come. That is the most important thing!

Kill What Is Dear to You

When the Levites decided to go to where Moses was, they were also making the decision to forsake all eleven of the other tribes of Israel. They actually left their family and friends to join with Moses. This had to be a hard thing to do. But what was even harder was what they were instructed to do next.

> Then he said to them, "This is what the Lord, the God of Israel, says: 'Each man strap a sword to his side. Go back and forth through the camp from one end to the other, each killing his brother and friend and neighbor.'" The Levites did as Moses commanded, and that day about three thousand of the people died.
>
> Exodus 32:27,28

The Levites were commanded to kill their own brothers, sisters, friends and neighbors. They had spent countless days with their fellow tribesmen, especially during their captivity in Egypt. They had experienced the joy of leaving Egypt together, and the miracle of crossing the Red Sea on dry ground. However, this was God's way of cleansing the evil from the entire camp.

21

For the Levites, their family, friends and neighbors were most near and dear to them, but they also represented idolatry against God. Anything or anyone who becomes a god to us, other than the true and living God, must be destroyed. Idolatry is an abomination to God, whether it be people or things. Nothing should ever stand in the way of our relationship with God, or the call He has placed on our lives.

What are those things that could be considered idols in our lives? God is asking us to search the camp of our heart, mind and soul, and kill whatever could ultimately cause us to be separated from Him. Colossians 3:5-10 encourages us to mortify or put to death the deeds of the flesh. This is not an easy thing. I'm sure it wasn't easy for the Levites. But like with the Levites, God wants to make sure there is no evil in our camp. We have to be willing to destroy those things that are holding us back. If we kill these things, then we have moved one step closer to qualifying for ministry unto the Lord.

Be Thoroughly Cleansed

Before the Levites could do any work in the temple they had to be cleansed.

> **The Lord said to Moses: "Take the Levites from among the other Israelites and make them ceremonially clean. To purify them, do this: Sprinkle the water of cleansing on them; then have them shave their whole bodies and wash their clothes, and so purify themselves."**
>
> **Numbers 8:5-7**

Water is symbolic of the Holy Spirit. After we have made the initial decision to follow Christ, the Holy Spirit comes to finish the work, cleansing us from dead works. This is our spiritual coronation. We are officially set aside, thoroughly washed, and anointed for service. The purification process which the Levites went through did not just happen once. They were purified each time they were to enter the temple for service (Exodus 40:32). Likewise, the purification process the Holy Spirit takes us through is continual. It doesn't just happen once. We need to be spiritually cleansed each time we are to minister in a service.

The shaving of the body hair is another outward sign of separation from the world. It also symbolizes total submission to God by laying aside every weight and sin which does so easily beset us (Hebrews 12:1). We often become dusty or dirty from being in this world, even though we are not of this world. The Holy Spirit teaches us how to wash and shave in order to be ready for temple service. It is up to us to submit daily to this cleansing process.

> **Therefore, brothers, since we have confidence to enter the Most Holy Place by the blood of Jesus, by a new and living way opened for us through the curtain, that is, his body, and since we have a great priest over the house of God, let us draw near to God with a sincere heart in full assurance of faith, having our hearts sprinkled to cleanse us from a guilty conscience and having our bodies washed with pure water.**
>
> **Hebrews 10:19-22**

There are two major areas in our lives which require continual purification. First, those things we think on or ponder in our heart, and secondly, the things we actually do. Unless these areas are purified, we cannot enter into the service of the temple. David asked a very important question as it related to his personal desire to be accepted into God's presence.

> **Who shall ascend into the hill of the Lord? or who shall stand in his holy place?**
>
> **Psalm 24:3** KJV

David wanted to know who could actually be where God dwelt. Who can stand or serve in the house of the Lord? As it relates to us, what type of person is fit to minister in the holy place? David records the answer in the next verse.

> **He that hath clean hands, and a pure heart; who hath not lifted up his soul unto vanity, nor sworn deceitfully.**
>
> **Psalm 24:4** KJV

God gave David four different answers to his one question. The first two are to have clean hands and a pure heart. This represents both our deeds and the motives behind our deeds—what we do, and why we do it. Our deeds can be no purer than the motives behind them. Are there hidden reasons for wanting to render service in the temple? Our motives will determine whether we are accepted in the holy place.

The third requirement speaks of any idols we may have hidden away in our lives. Again, idols represent people or things we value more than our relationship with God. We can never enter into the most holy place if there are other idols we are bowing to. The fourth requirement is the truthfulness of the vow we have made to God, which is closely related to our motives. Our vow to God can never be any more genuine than our motives. Our vow also cannot be genuine if we have not removed all of the idols from our lives.

God's reply to David was simple. Let everything you do and think be clean and pure. Make sure there

24

are no idols in your life. Be truthful and unwavering in your vow to Him.

This idea of purification is not a state of being, but rather a process of becoming. Our motives and deeds are continually being purified for service. God has already provided grace for our many blunders and mistakes. Although we are not perfect, the key is to always strive for "pure-fection" in Him. Be willing to submit to the Holy Spirit's many washings and shavings during this process.

Carry the Burden

After the Levites were ceremonially cleansed, there were specific duties they were required to fulfill before they could sing or serve in any ministerial capacity.

> **After you have purified the Levites and presented them as a wave offering, they are to come to do their work at the Tent of Meeting.**
>
> **Numbers 8:15**

Before the Levites were able to minister in the temple, they had to set up the tent and properly arrange the furniture. They had to carry in all the temple articles, making sure everything was properly placed. The fourth chapter of Numbers describes the Levites' duties of carrying the temple articles. The three families which were from the three sons of Levi, each had something different to carry. Numbers 4:49 states, "At the Lord's command through Moses, each was assigned his work and told what to carry."

This fourth chapter of Numbers begins by describing what the Kohathites had to carry. They were responsible for carrying the most holy things (v. 4). This included the ark of testimony, the lamp stand, the table of shewbread, and all the holy furnishings and articles within the temple and most holy place. They would never actually touch the temple articles, but were instructed to wrap them in blue cloth, cover them with badger's skin and put them in a special carrying frame (v. 12).

The Gershonites were responsible for carrying the curtains of the tabernacle and the Tent of Meeting (vv. 25,26). They were instructed to wrap the curtains in the same manner as the Kohathites. The Merarites were responsible for carrying the frames, crossbars, posts and anything else that pertained to the infrastructure of the tabernacle (vv. 31,32). They would also wrap everything in the prescribed manner.

The carrying of these temple articles by the Levites is symbolic of them having a burden for the ministry. In the same manner, before we can minister in the temple, we must have a burden for the area to which we are called. We can learn much from what each Levitical family had to carry.

The temple articles and furnishings the Kohathites carried represented the presence and anointing of God. Like the Kohathites, we should have a burden to see the presence and anointing of God manifested in our services for healing and deliverance. The curtains which the Gershonites carried comes from the Hebrew word *yara*, meaning to be broken or grievous.[3] As with the Gershonites, we should be grievous over hurting members in the congregation who need a touch from God. The pillars the Merarites carried comes from the Hebrew word *amad*, which means to appoint, to ordain or to confirm.[4] Like the Merarites, we should have a burden for the general infrastructure or framework of the church where we have been called and appointed to minister. Our call to minister cannot be separate from the vision of our local church and leadership.

Having a genuine burden for the ministry will always result in one thing—the desire to pray. This is the only way we can truly shoulder the burden we have for the ministry. In the same manner in which the Levites wrapped the temple articles in blue cloth and then badger's skin, the burden we carry must first be wrapped and tied in prayer, then covered by the Spirit. Anything carried in or by our flesh will be contaminated. It is rendered useless in the temple, and unacceptable to the Father. The burden we have for the ministry can only be carried in cloths made of effectual fervent prayers.

Have the Ability

God will never call us to something that He knows we don't have the ability to carry out. Not everyone can play an instrument. Not everyone can sing. If God has called you to the specific ministry of music, and you have a call and burden for that ministry, then no doubt you have been given the ability to perform the duties of that call. The Bible says that Kenaniah was put in charge of the singing, because he was skillful at it (1 Chronicles 15:22). All of the musicians and singers whom David chose were skillful enough to minister in song.

> **Along with their relatives—all of them trained and skilled in music for the Lord...**
>
> **1 Chronicles 25:7**

It should always be our desire to give God our best. For this reason, auditioning of singers and musicians is always in order. The purpose of an audition is not to weed out bad singers, or even to identify good singers. There will always be some who are more talented than others. The real purpose of an audition is to see if an individual has any potential in the area of music.

There are a lot of people who are called to sing, but just don't know it yet. Maybe, for some reason, they were discouraged from singing at a young age, or they just don't sing enough to realize how much potential they possess. When I audition singers I don't listen for perfection. I listen for potential. When I hear someone sing, and they have potential, this lets me know God has invested a musical gift in them. As minister of music, it is my job to draw that gift out of them so it can be nurtured to its fullest potential.

What do you do with a person who doesn't seem to have an ear for music? This is a hard question to answer. You don't want to discourage anyone from praising God. However, if it is up to me to draw out the musical gift of someone who has potential, it is also my responsibility to redirect a person who doesn't have musical potential in hope they will discover their true call. Again, we must give God our best. When He appoints, He equips and anoints.

There have been occasions when I have tried to help a person discover their true call because they did not have an ear for music. I sometimes instruct them to work on some things vocally, and then invite them to audition again at a later date. If after the second audition there is still no display of potential, I let them know that in my opinion their call is probably not to the music ministry.

You always want to be honest with people. If you allow someone in the choir who is unable to match tones, you make it difficult for others. In a sense you are actually allowing that person to be misguided in his or her pursuit to fulfill the correct call on their life.

And When They Began To Sing . . .

3

And Now a Selection From the Choir

In most churches today, both large and small, the major thrust of the music program is the choir ministry. The choir ministry plays a major role in assuring the congregation is edified and blessed during services. For this reason, it is important that every choir member understand their purpose. The central focus and vision for a choir ministry can easily be blurred into an ineffective time of entertainment, if its underlying purpose is anything different from that which God originally designed. Myles Munroe says, "When you don't know the purpose of a thing, abuse is eminent."There are many choirs who are suffering from abuse, because they have been abnormally used. They are ineffective, because they haven't understood their purpose as a choir ministry. One way to discover this purpose is to study just what a choir is.

What does the word *choir* really mean? It is defined as "a body of trained singers or that part of a church occupied by them; any band or organized company of dancers or singers."[5] According to this standard definition, a choir is a body, a band, an organized company of trained singers. It is a group of people working toward the same goal. This definition denotes oneness, unity, and togetherness. The word *band*, as used in this definition, further emphasizes this togetherness. It is defined as a company of persons associated, organized, or bound together.[6] A choir has a common thread of association, one point of identification that solidifies them as a distinguished or set aside group. They are joined together for one purpose. If this togetherness or unity is not present, by definition it is not a choir.

Possessing the attributes of this definition, however, is merely the beginning. The dictionary only describes the physical characteristics of a choir. We must also look at the spiritual characteristics of the choir. For it is in the Spirit that there is life and liberty. If a choir has no spiritual meaning or significance, there is only dead togetherness.

Although the word *choir* is the term most commonly used today when describing a large group of singers, it is actually never mentioned in the *King James Version* of the Bible. The word generally used is *singers*. This word is used to describe both musicians and choir members. The Hebrew translation for the word singers is shuwr, which is pronounced shoor.[7] This word has four distinct meanings, which are as follows:

1. To sing or stroll like a minstrel

2. To turn or travel about

3. Going around for inspection

4. A wall

A close look at each of these definitions will help us better understand God's original intent for the choir ministry.

To Sing or Stroll Like a Minstrel

This first definition represents the more basic and

fundamental meaning of singers. When one or more people sing, they are simply uttering words or sounds with musical inflections of the voice or instrument. These sounds are uttered when air moves up through the windpipe and passes over the vocal chords causing them to vibrate. This constant vibration of the vocal chords produces a sound or tone which comes out of the mouth. This simple process provides us with a common theme that will be evident in each definition of singers we discuss. Look once again at the process of singing. Notice these key action words and phrases: moves up, passes over, vibration and comes out. All of these words denote some type of movement. Singing is an action word. There is always some type of movement associated with music. The above process describes physical movement, but there is also movement that takes place in the Spirit when a choir begins to sing.

Have you ever heard someone say, "That was a real moving song"? It was because there was something about the song, and those who sang it, that caused a reaction in the listeners' emotions and spirit. It touched their heart strings. The movement or vibration of a song causes a reaction in the innermost parts of our being.

Music, by voice or instrument, has the ability to not only tap into the Spirit realm, but also to command change in the Spirit. Do you remember when David played the harp for King Saul, who was vexed by an evil spirit? As David played his harp, 1 Samuel 16:23 (KJV) says, "...Saul was refreshed, and was well, and the evil spirit departed from him."

When a song is ministered in the right spirit (and we know that David was a man after God's own heart), it brings about positive change. It causes principalities to move. Just like the movement of physical air causes a vibration of sound, the movement of the Spirit in music causes a vibration of change. As singers, we must not only be aware of this movement, we must also be ready to move with the Spirit.

Strolling like a minstrel makes this idea of movement even clearer. It means to sing as you go, or go as you sing. During medieval times a minstrel would travel from town to town singing to the accompaniment of a harp or flute. The minstrel was able to affect more people through singing if he or she moved while they sang. As a matter of fact, 1 Samuel 18:6 is used to explain the root of this definition.

> **And it came to pass as they came, when David was returned from the slaughter of the Philistine, that the women came out of all cities of Israel, singing and dancing, to meet king Saul, with tabrets, with joy, and with instruments of music** (KJV).

These women strolled as they sang. They came from their various towns singing and dancing together with musical instruments. In this case the movement was more for celebration. However, this is not the only type of movement described in the definition of shuwr. It can also be mournful, defensive, or offensive. This means that when we sing, we should be aware of the occasion, and adjust or move towards that purpose. A choir must be aware of what is taking place in the spiritual realm while they are singing, and be ready to move if necessary.

To Turn or Travel About

This definition sheds further light on the unique characteristics and function of a choir from a spiritual standpoint. Here singers are likened to both a harlot and a merchant, who each for different reasons are always on the go, turning and traveling from place to place. Usually when a person turns, he is turning his attention from one thing to another. At one point in time, he was focused on one thing, but then something else caught his eye. This causes him to turn and travel toward whatever it was that got his attention.

A harlot or prostitute is always on the go. She is constantly turning from one paying customer to another. A merchant or traveling salesman is also going from place to place, turning here and there, in an attempt to sell his goods. But how does this relate to a choir? What causes the singers to turn and travel about? Where are the singers going?

Going Around for Inspection

The idea of movement is evident in this definition as well. Singers are to move around a particular area with the intent to inspect. An armed guard makes rounds on his watch. He doesn't stay in one place. He has an area that he must guard and inspect to make sure there are no hidden dangers or unwanted intruders. If there are, he must turn and move toward them with the intent of removing them from the premises.

As we look closer at this particular Hebrew definition, we find that it more specifically means to spy out, to survey, to lurk for evil, to care for good, to lay wait, to observe, to perceive, and to see.[8] It is the choir's responsibility to go around for inspection. This is done by taking a spiritual survey of the area they are assigned to protect. They are to be on watch for evil, while at the same time caring for the good. Singers are to be spiritually alert and on guard, discerning the spiritual environment around them.

I am reminded of Jesus' instructions to His disciples in the garden of Gethsemane. He told them to "Watch and pray..." (Matthew 26:41). Jesus could feel the demons of death hovering over Him like vultures. He knew that it was just a matter of time before He would have to temporarily surrender to them. He was overwhelmed and sorrowful almost to the point of death. He could sense death all around Him. Even at this most desperate time in His earthly life, Jesus wanted to teach His disciples one last lesson. He wanted them to be aware of the evil around them. He told them to be on watch, not so much for His sake, but for theirs. Peter never forgot this very serious episode with Jesus, and even hints of its effects on his life when he wrote,

> **Be self-controlled and alert. Your enemy the devil prowls around like a roaring lion looking for someone to devour. Resist him, standing firm in the faith, because you know that your brothers throughout the world are undergoing the same kind of sufferings.**

> **1 Peter 5:8,9**

It is every choir member's responsibility to be spiritually alert in order to have any kind of defense against the attacks and sabotage of the enemy. Peter states two things. First, be sober enough to identify the devil and his tricks. Second, once you have identified the evil, resist it. James stated, "...Resist the devil, and he will flee from you"(James 4:7). I used to think this idea of resisting the devil simply meant to reject or turn away from what he was offering. When a salesman comes to your door, you can say "no thank you, I'm not interested," as you close the door. This may work on a salesman, but not on the devil.

The word *resist* in the New Testament means to stand against, oppose, or withstand.[9] It is taken from the Greek root word *anti*, which means opposite. This is a familiar term in the English language. Most of us have had an opposing view of something. We all should be opposed to or anti-devil. When the devil comes to our door, we don't just say "no thank you," and close the door. We violently remove him from our property, and our neighborhood as well.

In the same manner, a choir must firmly stand in opposition against whatever the devil may try to "sell" to God's people, violently opposing him until he flees. They must resist the devil in order to ensure the good is cared for and protected. The "good" is the Word of God, and His people. The congregation is under attack during a church service, because the devil doesn't want the Word of God to fall on good ground. The devil is constantly trying to see who he can distract, defeat and ultimately destroy. It is the choir's responsibility, through their ministry in song, to care for the congregation by getting rid of all the distractions. This ultimately clears the path for complete deliverance in the service.

When a choir stands to sing in a service, many things are set in motion in the spirit realm. Any evil spirits present immediately recognize they are about to be assaulted. They will try to distract the listener by tightening the grips of oppression and depression. Demons know the power of anointed music. They experienced it in heaven. Their leader Satan was created to bring forth music to the glory of God.

Demons know that if the listener receives the Word
of Truth through music, they will be set free, and they
will have to flee. The demon does all he can to make
sure the listener cannot receive his or her deliverance.
When a choir begins to sing, it is this battle they must
"turn" their spiritual attention to. Any evil present must
be uprooted by the choir. The choir, in the spirit, is
searching out their territory, which is the congregation.
Any evil is considered an unwanted intruder, and must
be expelled.

The singers must collectively go around for inspection, and be ready to go to battle against the enemy.

> **For we wrestle not against flesh and blood, but
> against principalities, against powers, against the
> rulers of the darkness of this world, against spiritual
> wickedness in high places.**
>
> **Ephesians 6:12 KJV**

The fact is we do wrestle. It's not against people,
but against evil forces we cannot see with our physical
eyes. It is a spiritual battle. Each individual choir
member must sing with this purpose in mind, that they
are sending forth deliverance to God's people. As they
sing praises to the Lord, He is setting ambushes which
are targeted for those principalities who have dared to
trespass on holy ground.

The choir is singing boldly with strength and
authority, realizing the power of God is setting captives
free. In Ephesians 6:13-18 Paul goes on to describe how
we are to fight against the devil by putting on the whole
armor of God. The choir is an army that must be well
prepared in order to defeat its enemy. There can be no
breaking of ranks, no insubordination, and no soldiers
going spiritually AWOL. This army must fight as one.

The deliverance of God's people depends on it. An unprepared army, or an army that doesn't know why it is fighting, is assured of defeat.

Paul says one last thing right after he describes the armor, which further emphasizes the importance of a choir's duty to inspect its territory. In Ephesians 6:18 he instructs the Church to watch with infinite endurance for all saints: ". . . be alert and always keep on praying for all the saints." We must remember that an army is necessary for the protection of the people, not just for ourselves. Therefore, when a choir sings they are going out on the front line of the spirit realm, representing the congregation. They must watch and be alert lest the enemy ambush God's people.

A Wall

The fourth definition or characteristic of a choir is a wall. In general, a wall encloses or encircles that which it desires to protect. It separates one thing from another, usually for the purpose of protection. The choir ministry serves as a wall of protection from evil on behalf of the good. They shield the congregation from any evil forces. This wall is built so high nothing can get over it. It is so deeply rooted in the spirit nothing can go under it, and so thick with the anointing nothing can go through it. A choir should be so tightly knit spiritually that nothing can penetrate its wall of defense. The enemy will definitely try to get through it. That's why it is so important there be no holes or gaps in the wall. The choir ministry must be united and spiritually consistent so nothing can permeate its wall.

Every choir member must have the same vision, and must speak and sing as one united force. The devil and his demons will constantly scale the wall trying to find the slightest opening. They will try to push against it to see how strong it is. A choir must withstand the pressure and adversity in order to gain a spiritual victory. They must be a spiritual fortress that will not be infiltrated. If the devil can get in by causing division, he will. If he can knock a hole in the wall with gossip, he will. He will stop at nothing to break through that wall of protection.

A great example of a choir demonstrating the characteristics of a wall is found in 2 Chronicles 20. This chapter begins with a vast army making war against King Jehoshaphat. The king prayed and then received a word from the Lord through Jahaziel in verses 15 and 16.

> **Do not be afraid or discouraged because of this vast army. For the battle is not yours, but God's. Tomorrow march down against them. . . .**

I love that last statement, because it shows that God wants a choir that is spiritually aggressive toward the enemy. That's easy to do once you realize the battle is not yours, but God's. He just wants you to be in the right place at the right time, to do exactly what He says, when He says, because then and only then is victory inevitable.

Following the prophecy, Jehoshaphat and all of Israel had a church service. The Levites led the praise and worship. This put Israel in the right frame of mind and spirit to march against their enemies. The next morning they set out toward the enemy. Notice what King Jehoshaphat's instructions were. He appointed singers to sing as they marched toward the enemy. Remember, a choir must be ready to move. The singers went out ahead of the army.

> **After consulting the people, Jehoshaphat appointed men to sing to the Lord and to praise him for the splendor of his holiness as they went out at the head of the army, saying: "Give thanks to the Lord, for his love endures forever."**
>
> **2 Chronicles 20:21**

The choir marched as a wall of protection for those who carried the weapons. It was the choir who ensured safe passage for those with swords. Ephesians 6:17 tells us the sword of the Spirit is the Word of God, and the pastor is the one who delivers this Word. It is the choir's responsibility to go before the pastor and clear the way for the Word with anointed and powerful praise to the Lord. They must march forward spiritually and advance toward the enemy. As with King Jehoshaphat, the result will always be complete and decisive victory!

> **As they began to sing and praise, the Lord set ambushes against the men of Ammon and Moab and Mount Seir who were invading Judah, and they were defeated.**
>
> **2 Chronicles 20:22**

As the praises go forth, God is the One Who actually fights the battle. The choir's only responsibility is to be united as one, a wall-like fortress advancing toward the enemy. When the choir does this, there is no place for the devil to go, but out!

Paul stated in Ephesians 4:27, "Neither give place to the devil"(KJV). The word *place* in Greek is topos, which means a spot, a location, an opportunity, or license.[10] The word *topos* is where we get the English word *topography. Topography* is a description of the physical features of a region. It describes the various physical characteristics of an entire neighborhood.[11]

I believe what Paul was saying was, "Don't even allow the devil into your neighborhood." As a collective body of singers, a choir cannot allow the devil into their spiritual territory.

Paul knew the devil was very territorial. He still is! He will try to take advantage of every little space we leave open. This is why it is important for the choir to understand its purpose and role as a collective body advancing toward the enemy. The choir is to be an anointed musical fortress, clearing the path for the deliverance of God's people.

4

Choir's Attire

What should a choir wear when they minister in the house of the Lord? Should each choir member wear the same thing? The choirs during King David's time did.

> **Now David was clothed in a robe of fine linen, as were all the Levites who were carrying the ark, and as were the singers, and Kenaniah, who was in charge of the singing of the choirs.**
>
> **1 Chronicles 15:27**

The entire choir wore the same thing, which happened to be a type of garment made of white linen. It must have looked beautiful. White is symbolic of purity and integrity. I'm in no way suggesting that all choirs wear white. I'm not even suggesting that a choir always wear the same colored garment. It really doesn't matter what the choir wears externally. "Man looks at the outward appearance, but the Lord looks at the heart" (1 Samuel 16:7).

The outward adorning of a choir is only significant to the extent that it reflects the inward adorning. It is not important what a choir wears on the outside, if they are not wearing the same thing on the inside. What should a choir wear when they minister in the house of the Lord? Should each choir member wear the same thing? Absolutely, positively, YES!

43

We have already seen how the choir is a spiritual army. With this in mind, let's look at the armor of a soldier in order to gain some insight as to what the attire of a choir should be. In Ephesians chapter 6, Paul mentions six pieces of armor which help to both protect the soldier, and attack the enemy. In relating this armor to a choir, I believe the most important piece of armor is the belt of truth. The belt is what holds the other pieces of armor in place. It keeps everything together and secure.

Truth is the only thing that can hold a choir together. Not just any kind of truth, but the real Truth. Jesus said, "I am the way, the truth, and the life..." (John 14:6 KJV). He is the truth. Every aspect of Jesus, every characteristic of Jesus is founded upon truth. A choir must operate in this truth if it is to be effective in ministry. When a choir fails to operate in truth, their worship is fruitless, and their power for deliverance is negated. In John 4:23,24 Jesus said,

> But the hour cometh, and now is, when the true worshippers shall worship the Father in spirit and in truth: for the Father seeketh such to worship him. God is a Spirit: and they that worship him must worship him in spirit and in truth (KJV).

We, as believers, have seemingly mastered the art of worshipping God in spirit, while we ignore the importance of dealing in truth. Our worship is incomplete without this main ingredient. The word *truth* or *true* is defined as something that is not concealed, accurate, verified, certified, correct, valid, loyal, reliable, sincere, genuine, authentic, pure and real.[12] All of these are characteristics each choir member must have toward one another in order to operate in truth. Where there is truth, division cannot reside. Division cannot manifest itself in truth.

When a choir fails to operate in truth, division will always be present. As a result, the worship is without integrity. Instead of being accurate it misses the spiritual target. Instead of being certified, it has no seal of God's approval. Instead of being pure, it is tainted. When a choir operates in this false realm, the congregation is simply being entertained. The ultimate objective is never reached.

When a choir operates in truth, the congregation identifies with that truth, which leads to their deliverance. Jesus said, "And ye shall know the truth, and the truth shall make you free" (John 8:32 KJV). This is the truth we experience as a result of our knowledge of, and relationship with, Jesus Christ.

The truth of God must be in operation between our fellow brothers and sisters if our collective praise is to be effective. In Psalm 15 David asked the Lord an interesting question. We as singers must ask ourselves this same question if we are to wear the same attire.

> **Lord, who shall abide in thy tabernacle? who shall dwell in thy holy hill?**
>
> Psalm 15:1 KJV

As ministers in music, it should be our desire for the praises we offer to God to ascend to the holy hill of the Lord. What must we do to ensure the Lord receives our praise? What must we do to ensure our place in the tabernacle of the Lord?

> **He that walketh uprightly, and worketh righteousness, and speaketh the truth in his heart.**
>
> Psalm 15:2 KJV

Our Christian walk and works of righteousness will always affect those around us. When our relationship with the Father is healthy and in focus, our relationships with one another will also tend to be healthy. This ultimately leads to truthful communication.

When we speak, we are directly communicating and interacting with another person. We cannot speak or converse with someone without having a direct affect on their life. Our spoken words will have either a positive or negative affect on those who hear them. Solomon wrote in Proverbs 18:21,

> **Death and life are in the power of the tongue: and they that love it shall eat the fruit thereof** (KJV).

The writer James devotes an entire chapter to the power and dangers of the tongue. Read the third chapter of James to capture the full scope of his message. Allow me to briefly summarize the chapter. In the first few verses James compares the tongue to the small bit that is put in a horse's mouth, and also the helm of a large ship. Both of these small things determine the direction the horse and ship will go respectively. James goes on to say in verse 6 that the tongue is a fire, and has the power to burn up or defile the whole body. In other words, one unbridled tongue has the potential to go through and destroy an entire choir, much like a wild fire burns a forest.

James then says that although man has been able to tame all kinds of beasts, he has not been able to tame his own tongue, because it is unruly, and full of deadly poison (vv. 7,8). Another major concern of James is the inherent hypocritical nature of the tongue, which is able to send forth both words of sweetness and curses of bitterness at the same time. James gives a quick prelude to this third chapter in James 1:26,

> **If anyone considers himself religious and yet does not keep a tight rein on his tongue, he deceives himself and his religion is worthless.**

Everything we seek to accomplish in the choir ministry is utterly paralyzed if we cannot individually win the battle over the control of our tongue. I have seen many choirs destroyed because of seeds of destruction and division planted by a few of its members. If a choir is to ascend to that place David spoke of, we must learn how to speak only the truth to one another. We can't speak what we've heard from someone else. That is gossip, and it only helps to spread the wildfire. We can't speak based on speculation, because it is not confirmed truth, and tends to plant seeds of doubt in the minds of those who hear it. We cannot even speak what we feel, unless it is under the unction of the Holy Spirit, because we are allowing our emotions to rule our tongue rather than the Spirit of God. James, the obvious authority on the dangers of the tongue, encourages us to "be swift to hear, slow to speak, slow to wrath" (James 1:19 KJV).

As choir members, we must learn to speak only life and encouragement to one another. If we can do this, then and only then do we qualify to abide in the tabernacle of God's presence. Referring back to Psalm 15, David gives an additional answer to the question he posed in verse one.

> **He that backbiteth not with his tongue, nor doeth evil to his neighbour, nor taketh up a reproach against his neighbour.**
>
> **Psalm 15:3 KJV**

Your fellow choir member is your neighbor. God is not pleased when we sing praises to Him, but can't get along with or speak well of the person who is standing right next to us. We cannot minister truth as a choir, if we don't operate in truth on a regular basis. God desires truth in the "inward parts" (Psalm 51:6 KJV).

5

Stop the Music!

Have you ever been in a church service where after the choir finished singing you sensed something just wasn't right? They sounded good vocally, but there was a distinct absence of God's anointing on their ministry? Your spirit man would not allow you to join in, or receive what was being presented?

You may have had an idea of what the problem was. Maybe you sensed something was not right with the music director. Maybe the style of the song was not appropriate for church, and thus did not bring glory to the Lord. Maybe the choir was having some serious problems with division among its members and leadership. It quite possibly could have been any combination of the above. One thing is for sure, any or all of the above situations can slowly drain God's anointing from a music ministry. If steps are not taken to deal with these issues, the devil will ultimately receive more gratification from the singing than the Lord and His people.

When music in a church is performed for the wrong reasons or by the wrong people, it ceases to be edifying. When this happens, adjustments should be made to ensure that the music in a service is spiritually edifying to all those who are listening. Until this happens, the music should stop! This of course does not mean that you shut down the entire music department. It does mean that you change or remove those elements which hinder the flow of God's anointing.

There are three basic reasons why the music of a choir or band may need to be temporarily stopped until the proper personnel or musical material can be found.

The Wrong Music Director

The music director is the one who is responsible for all the music within a church. He or she will usually decide what songs will be sung during an entire service, which includes praise and worship, special choir songs, solos, and instrumentals. The music director, for the most part, sets the spiritual atmosphere in the service. The choir and band will generally follow the music director's lead. The overall effectiveness of the music ministry is determined by the music director. If the music director has not truly submitted to the lordship of Christ or the leadership of the pastor, this can cause mass confusion and division within the choir, and ultimately the congregation. This is exactly what took place in heaven.

When I was a little boy in church I used to hear preachers say that Satan was the choir director in heaven. This of course always got my attention, because I wanted to be a choir director. I just had a real problem with wanting to be like Satan. As I grew and began to study the validity of this statement, I realized that although there is no biblical evidence of him actually being a choir director, he was definitely heavily involved in the music in heaven. There are very few descriptions of Satan or Lucifer in the Bible. However, the few we find give some insight as to what Lucifer's responsibilities were during his time in heaven. The word *Lucifer* actually appears only once in the Bible.

> **How art thou fallen from heaven, O Lucifer, son of the morning! how art thou cut down to the ground, which didst weaken the nations!**
>
> **Isaiah 14:12 KJV**

Literally, this passage describes the overthrow of a tyrant, the king of Babylon. But many Bible scholars see in this passage a description of Satan, who rebelled against the throne of God and was "brought down to the grave, to the depths of the pit" (Isaiah 14:15).[13] Notice in verse 11 that Lucifer is described as having viols or harps. This gives some indication that he was specifically created by God for musical purposes. His name *Lucifer* in its original Hebrew translation is the word *halal*. This is the same Hebrew word that is used to define praise.[14] It appears Lucifer was the halal in heaven.

There is one other passage that seemingly describes many of Lucifer's characteristics. The prophet Ezekiel goes into great detail in describing this archangel Lucifer. Remember, it was God Who created him. Anything that God creates is going to be indescribably ornate and beautiful. There is no doubt in my mind that Lucifer was one of the most beautiful musical angels in all heaven. In looking at Ezekiel's description in chapter 28 we can see just how beautiful and musical he was.

> **This is what the Sovereign Lord says: "You were the model of perfection, full of wisdom and perfect in beauty. You were in Eden, the garden of God; every precious stone adorned you: ruby, topaz and emerald, chrysolite, onyx and jasper, sapphire, turquoise and beryl. Your settings and mountings were made of**

gold; on the day you were created they were prepared."

Ezekiel 28:12,13

God created Lucifer so perfect that he was looked
upon by all the other angels as the model by which they
should be compared. Every precious stone you could
imagine was inset into his body. These stones were set
in and around gold tabrets and pipes, which is the *King
James Translation* of settings and mountings. The tabret
was a percussion instrument much like the modern-day
tambourine. The use of the word *pipes*, which is a
type of wind instrument, suggests that Lucifer had the
ability to make sounds similar to a trumpet or possibly
even a pipe organ. The viols and harps as mentioned
in Isaiah 14:11 suggest he had musical strings attached
to his body, which enabled him to sound like a violin,
harp, or cello.

Take a moment, and try to imagine the numerous
musical possibilities Lucifer had. He was a walking,
floating philharmonic orchestra. He was uniquely
created to give praise and glory to God.

You were anointed as a guardian cherub, for so
I ordained you. You were on the holy mount of God;
you walked among the fiery stones.

Ezekiel 28:14

Lucifer was in such close proximity to God's throne
when God breathed, His breath would blow through
Lucifer's pipes and make the most beautiful music. The
light of God would reflect off Lucifer's many stones,
creating a wonderful and breathtaking laser light show.
The other angels could hear and see Lucifer coming from
afar, because of his indescribable music and reflective
beauty. He was the major source of music in heaven.

Because of the way God created him, Lucifer couldn't walk without giving praise to God. He couldn't fly without giving praise to God. He couldn't even breathe without praising God. Everything he did brought praise and glory to the one who created him, and he enjoyed it. He could have quite possibly been the minister of music in heaven. He was held in very high esteem by his peers.

> **You were blameless in your ways from the day you were created till wickedness was found in you. Through your widespread trade you were filled with violence, and you sinned. So I drove you in disgrace from the mount of God, and I expelled you, O guardian cherub, from among the fiery stones. Your heart became proud on account of your beauty, and you corrupted your wisdom because of your splendor. So I threw you to the earth; I made a spectacle of you before kings.**
>
> **Ezekiel 28:15-17**

Jesus remembered that fateful day. He gave His disciples a brief account of what happened: "I saw Satan fall like lightning from heaven" (Luke 10:18). Lucifer became lifted up in pride. He began to look at his endless beauty and talents rather than on the One Who created him. Lucifer's motives changed. He wanted to be like God. He failed to submit himself to his ultimate authority.

As a result, God dismissed him, along with a host of angels whom Lucifer was able to influence. God not only relieved Lucifer of his duties, He also cast him out of heaven. God fired His main source of music and praise. Think about it, for a brief period of time, heaven was without a minister of music. No longer could you hear the beautiful sounds of Lucifer on the mountain of

God. No longer could you see his magnificent light presentations.

With all of the beauty, gifts and talents Lucifer possessed, he became useless to the Kingdom. God had to stop his music. All heaven was affected, because the minister of music had the wrong spirit. So here is a question for pastors: if God Almighty can do without His main source of music in heaven for a season, can't you? There is never a time when we should put talents and gifts above character and integrity. I have been in churches where the minister of music was a practicing homosexual. At other churches, I have seen music directors who, by their actions, made sure everyone knew they were the star of the show. I have often observed a music director's negative attitude and disrespect for his pastor, while at the same time operating a dictatorship over the choir.

God is not pleased with this type of music director, and will not place His blessing on any music that comes from this type of spirit. It is detrimental to the pastor, the music ministry, and the congregation. We must follow the example of our heavenly Father, Who would not settle for a minister of music who was simply gifted and talented. His standards of clean hands (deeds), and a pure heart (motives), must also be ours. If God can make changes and adjustments in His music program to ensure that His praise is pure, then so can we.

It wasn't long after Lucifer's dismissal that God created you and me to take his place. He created us with hands to clap and raise in praise to Him. He gave us vocal chords (strings) to sing His praises. He also made us lively stones, so that when the light of His presence shines on us, we show forth His praises (1 Peter 2:5,9).

Now that's a light show. We are now, and forevermore, God's ministers of music. Praise God!

The Wrong Choir Member(s)

It is the responsibility of the music director, with the help of the pastor, to ensure that people who want to be choir members have a real heart and desire to minister to the Lord. Prospective choir members who have wrong motives, or unresolved personal issues, need first to be ministered to before they can be effective in ministering to others. Allowing people with the wrong motives or the wrong spirit to enter the choir will weaken the overall effectiveness of the music ministry.

Choir members who have problems with jealousy, gossiping, low self-esteem, envy and the like, can cause division in the choir. A choir member who has difficulty submitting to leadership should not be allowed in the choir. God originally intended for the music ministry to be a sacred, pure, and holy ministry. It should remain as clean as He originally intended it to be. If it is not, we must stop the music until the proper adjustments can be made. This is exactly what Nehemiah did.

From the time of the children of Israel's exodus from Egypt, God set specific guidelines for them to follow to ensure they would not be contaminated with evil from other nations. There were certain people and nations whom God expressly forbid them from dwelling with or marrying. He also forbid Israel's enemies from joining with them in worship. God knew that if He allowed this, it would eventually lead to the mixing of religious practices, and ultimately idolatry. An example of this was God's order to stay clear of any Moabites or Ammonites.

> No Ammonite or Moabite or any of his
> descendants may enter the assembly of the Lord, even
> down to the tenth generation. For they did not come
> to meet you with bread and water on your way when
> you came out of Egypt, and they hired Balaam son of
> Beor from Pethor in Aram Naharaim to pronounce a
> curse on you.
>
> Deutronomy 23:3-6

The Ammonites and Moabites were a long standing enemy of the Lord's, because they did not assist
Israel during their journey from Egypt. He did not want
them to ever set foot in His assembly. They were not of
the same kindred spirit as the children of Israel. The
Ammonites and Moabites worshipped Baal. In addition,
their origin was rooted in incest.

In Genesis 19:30-38 we find the birth of these tribes,
who are direct descendants of Lot. After Lot and his
two daughters fled from Sodom and Gomorrah, they
settled in a cave in the mountains of Zoar. Lot's two
daughters began to think they would never be with a
man in order to keep their family's bloodline alive. So
on two separate occasions they made their father drunk
and had intercourse with him.

> So both of Lot's daughters became pregnant by
> their father. The older daughter had a son, and she
> named him Moab; he is the father of the Moabites of
> today. The younger daughter also had a son, and she
> named him Ben-Ammi; he is the father of the
> Ammonites of today.
>
> Genesis 19:36-38

The ancestral bloodline of both the Moabites and
Ammonites was rooted in sexual immorality. It was this
type of spirit the Lord did not want in His most sacred
assembly. This is very significant, because years later

Nehemiah had to confront this same spirit.

In Nehemiah chapter 2, Nehemiah rallied all Israel together to rebuild the wall of Jerusalem. As they began the work, three arch rivals came against them, and tried to discourage them from rebuilding the wall. These three men were Sanballat, Tobiah, and Geshem (Nehemiah 2:9). There are many spiritual truths we can gain from the study of all three of these enemies. Of these three enemies, Tobiah is probably mentioned more than the other two foes. He was the most outspoken. It was Tobiah who outwardly mocked Nehemiah when he first mentioned rebuilding the wall (Nehemiah 4:3). He also sent letters to intimidate Nehemiah (Nehemiah 6:19). Tobiah was an Ammonite.

The wall of Jerusalem was built despite the efforts of Tobiah and his cohorts. When the wall was finished, Nehemiah organized a celebration service to dedicate it to the Lord. A description of this dedication service is given in Nehemiah 12:27-43. The Levites were called and two choirs were assembled. The choirs, along with trumpeters and other musicians, sang and danced on top of the wall. Nehemiah was with them. Then they took the celebration into the house of God (Nehemiah 12:40). "The sound of rejoicing in Jerusalem could be heard far away" (Nehemiah 12:43). During this joyous celebration someone began to read from the book of Moses.

> On that day the Book of Moses was read aloud in the hearing of the people and there it was found written that no Ammonite or Moabite should ever be admitted into the assembly of God, because they had not met the Israelites with food and water but had hired Balaam to call a curse down on them.
>
> **Nehemiah 13:1,2**

All of Israel was put in remembrance of God's decree to them years ago. When they heard this they removed from the assembly all those of foreign descent. No doubt the one who read the scripture noticed some people who should not have been there. However, there was one foreigner in the assembly that only a few knew about.

> **Before this, Eliashib the priest had been put in charge of the storerooms of the house of our God. He was closely associated with Tobiah, and he had provided him with a large room formerly used to store the grain offerings and incense and temple articles, and also the tithes of grain, new wine and oil prescribed for the Levites, singers and gatekeepers, as well as the contributions for the priests.**
>
> **Nehemiah 13:4,5**

Nehemiah's long time enemy Tobiah the Ammonite was actually living in the house of God. To make matters worse, Eliashib had allowed him to stay in the storeroom that held all the articles of worship. These things had been moved out in order to make room for Tobiah. Included in these articles of worship was the oil, which represents the anointing. It would appear that the anointing was removed from the house of the Lord, in order to make room for an idolatrous and rebellious spirit, rooted in sexual immorality. The very things the Israelites used to praise God with were replaced with people, things, and spirits which were contrary to God. The very room set aside for the worship of God was turned into an habitation for sexual immorality and rebellion against God.

The word *Ammonite* is taken from the Hebrew root amam, which means to overshadow by huddling together. It also means to become dim, or hide.[15] When

you combine these two meanings, a more precise definition of *Ammonite* is a hidden huddling together which
overshadows and makes dim. This is a perfect description of a clique. A smaller group within a larger group,
having a private agenda to tear down anyone outside
of their little circle. Cliques are divisive in nature. You
can't always see them, but you know that they are there.
They overshadow and cause the overall brightness of
God's glory to become dim. This is one type of spirit
which had taken up residence in the temple of the Lord.

When Nehemiah heard what had been taking place,
he stopped the celebration.

> **Here I learned about the evil thing Eliashib had
> done in providing Tobiah a room in the courts of the
> house of God. I was greatly displeased and threw all
> Tobiah's household goods out of the room. I gave
> orders to purify the rooms, and then I put back into
> them the equipment of the house of God, with the
> grain offerings and the incense.**
>
> **Nehemiah 13:7-9**

This evil thing made Nehemiah sick to his stomach. The thought that articles of praise had actually been
taken out of the house of God, and had been replaced
with all kinds of evil, was too much for Nehemiah to
bear. He considered this an evil thing, because it was in
total disobedience to God. I love Nehemiah's response.
He did three things many of us as pastors and music
directors might need to do in our ministries. First, he
threw out all of Tobiah's household goods. The *King
James* translates *household goods* as "stuff." Secondly, he
ordered the room to be thoroughly cleansed and purified. Nehemiah did not want even the stench of evil in
God's room. Thirdly, he put the room back in order. The

praise articles and the anointing were returned to the house of God.

Nehemiah had no tolerance for the wrong spirit in the house of God. He made those around him accountable to follow God's holy ordinances, in order to ensure that proper praise and worship would take place. If you have allowed a spirit of Tobiah in your music department, you can do no less than what Nehemiah did. Throw out the stuff, purify the rooms, and put back the anointing. We can't allow anything to hinder the flow of God's Spirit. With all the great singing and praising that took place during Israel's celebration, God could not have been pleased, because there was no place or provision for his anointing. The Bible says that God inhabits the praises of Israel (His people). However, God cannot inhabit our praise if we have "stuff" in the storerooms of our heart.

The Wrong Music

It is very easy to slip into the all too familiar trap of trying to please man with our music, rather than God. Many times we choose songs for a service based on the expected response from the congregation. We should be selecting music we feel will first bring glory to God, and secondly, edification to the congregation. When we begin to select our material based solely on the edification of the people, we begin to see a downward trend. The words and message of our songs are directed more toward the people rather than God, Who is the only One Who can deliver the people. The musical accompaniment is many times geared toward a style we know the people will respond favorably to. When our music fails to meet the first criteria of bringing praise and glory to God, we must stop the music until changes in our repertoire can be made. We see an example of this in 1 Samuel chapter 18. The music should have been stopped, but unfortunately, it wasn't. The end result was detrimental to all of Israel.

David had just killed Goliath. This was a feat that would have been considered a miracle even if it had been accomplished by a grown man. David was just a young lad, probably about sixteen years of age. His conquering of Goliath was a surprise to everyone. Because of David's great triumph over Goliath, the entire Philistine army fled, and Israel was able to claim victory. This was cause for a celebration. Upon returning from this great victory some singing and dancing ensued.

> **When the men were returning home after David had killed the Philistine, the women came out from all the towns of Israel to meet King Saul with singing and dancing, with joyful songs and with tambourines and lutes.**
>
> **1 Samuel 18:6**

These women were no doubt jubilant and energetic in their singing and dancing. They came from near and far, from all the surrounding towns of Israel just to greet, with songs of praise, the mighty men of war. However, there was something obviously wrong with their song selection.

> **As they danced, they sang: "Saul has slain his thousands, and David his tens of thousands."**
>
> **1 Samuel 18:7**

We know how this song made King Saul feel. He was very upset that these women would dare to compare him to a little boy. We don't really know how this song affected David. He was a young boy quickly thrown into a victory celebration as the hero.

But how did this celebration of song and dance make the Lord feel? Was it really King Saul and David who deserved the praise? No, it was the Lord Who caused David, and all Israel, to be victorious. So it is the Lord, and Him only, Who should have been the central focus of this celebration. God was definitely not pleased with this song, because it did not bring Him glory, and it was not edifying to *all* of Israel. They were singing to the wrong king. This is not at all surprising, since it was Israel who asked God for a king in the first place. However, this was not God's original plan for Israel.

> **But when they said, "Give us a king to lead us," this displeased Samuel; so he prayed to the Lord. And the Lord told him: "Listen to all that the people are saying to you; it is not you they have rejected, but they have rejected me as their king."**
>
> **1 Samuel 8:6,7**

This song the women sang was an outward sign of Israel's desire for an earthly king over that of their heavenly King. They were neglecting their true source of victory. Someone should have stopped the music, because it totally ignored the King of kings. This one song, and the failure to stop it, had a rippling adverse effect. King Saul became bitter toward David, and spent the rest of his reign trying to hunt him down to kill him. Poor David spent the next fifteen or so years dodging spears, fleeing for his life, living in and out of caves. The children of Israel suffered because their king became mad. They also lost the benefit of a key leader in the person of David for many years.

Nothing good can ever come out of music that is geared specifically toward the praise and glory of man, rather than the Creator of man. Our song selection for church services must always first give total glory to God. We cannot sing songs that make people wonder who the song is talking about. God was not pleased with this in David's day, and He is not pleased with it today.

And When They Began To Sing . . .

6
Is There Really Strength in Numbers?

There are many churches today, both large and small, that don't have a choir ministry as part of their music program. There are various reasons for this. Many pastors have opted, instead, for a smaller praise team of no more than about ten singers accompanied by a small band. (Although the definition of a choir does not specify a number, our assumption here, as is typically the case, is that a choir is much larger in number than that of a praise team.) Some pastors simply have not found a qualified person to be choir director. Other pastors don't see a need for a choir ministry in their church. For them, the praise team fills all the music needs in their church. This is due to the fact that the extent of their music is praise and worship, with a special solo here and there.

There are many pastors who would love to have a choir, but just don't want the headaches commonly associated with bringing together so many different attitudes and personalities on a weekly basis. For some pastors, a choir is not in their plans at all. But for others, a choir ministry is something they definitely want in the future. Their current praise team is a step toward this goal.

If a church is to have a choir ministry, the pastor must first have a vision for, and see a need for this ministry within his or her church. Unfortunately, not all pastors have this desire. However, there are a few questions we need to ask ourselves. Can a praise team take the place of, or accomplish the same things as a choir? Is the choir ministry necessary in light of the diversity and more simplistic makeup of the praise team? And finally, in comparing the choir ministry to the praise team ministry, is there really strength in numbers?

And the answers are...No! Yes!! Yes!!! I have nothing against the praise team ministry. I have worked with praise teams and smaller groups for most of my life. I personally enjoy the intimacy of these smaller groups. In the church where I am currently serving as Minister of Music, we have a separate weekly praise team rehearsal in addition to our weekly choir rehearsal. The praise team ministry is a vital and useful tool for any church, especially for a mid-week service or prayer meeting where the attendance is smaller. However, it can never take the place of the choir ministry, simply because they are totally different in their function. This is due mainly to the vast difference in the number of people who are typically used in the choir as opposed to the praise team.

God was always specific on matters concerning His temple, down to how many Levites should minister in song. In 1 Chronicles 23:5, David set aside four thousand to praise the Lord with musical instruments. In verse 31 of that same chapter we read, "They were to serve before the Lord regularly in the *proper number* and in the way prescribed for them." However, this group of four thousand did not all minister at the same time.

They ministered in shifts both day and night. A more distinct number is found in 1 Chronicles 25:7. They numbered two hundred and eighty-eight. Now that was a choir!

There is definitely strength in numbers. Not so much for the physical makeup, but rather for the overall spiritual effect it has on the enemy. The Lord is very clear on this matter. He knows large groups of people, united for the single purpose of advancing His Kingdom, are intimidating to the devil. Do you remember what God did when the devil sent an army with horses and chariots to capture Elisha? Elisha's reply to his nervous servant was simple, "Those who are with us are more than those who are with them" (2 Kings 6:16).

Remember, while we are giving praise to God, there are evil forces we are warring against in the spirit. The enemy doesn't want God to receive the praise, and he doesn't want the congregation to receive their deliverance, which often comes through the ministry of music. The number of singers we send out to battle will often determine the outcome. When King Jehoshaphat appointed singers to go before his army he did not send a praise team (2 Chronicles 20). He sent a large choir. They had to be very close in number to the army they were preceding.

The enemy is intimidated by united numbers. It is much harder for him to break through our spiritual barriers when we are many operating as one. That is why he tries so hard to divide us. He wants to reduce us down to size in hopes that he can somehow even the odds. In light of this, we must strive to incorporate the choir ministry into our churches whenever possible. There is a definite place and function for the praise team, but there is also a place, and a definite spiritual need, for the choir ministry. A choir singing as one, has a strength in terms of both volume and spirit that is hard to achieve with just a few singers. Now I ask you, if the enemy was coming against your church, like he came against Jehoshaphat's, would you rather send out ten singers who were united, or a hundred singers who were united?

> And ye shall chase your enemies, and they shall fall before you by the sword. And five of you shall chase an hundred, and an hundred of you shall put ten thousand to flight: and your enemies shall fall before you by the sword.
>
> Leviticus 26:7,8 KJV

7

How To Organize a Choir Ministry

Once the pastor senses the need for a choir ministry, he must first pray for the right leadership to lead the choir. If the praise team leader is already teaching vocal parts, he or she may also be able to lead the choir. Whoever the pastor chooses must be a people person with patience. If not, the choir will experience a constant turnover in membership. The person the pastor chooses should have a "corralling" type spirit. This is a gift for gathering together and motivating people for one purpose and goal. Once the proper leadership is in place, you are ready to organize your church choir. There are four basic steps to organizing a choir ministry. Let's briefly look at each one.

Step One: The Announcement

In this first step you want to make the congregation aware that a choir is being formed. You can do this by putting an announcement in your church bulletin, or you can make a special announcement during services. I would do both just to make certain everyone is notified. Not everyone reads the church bulletin, and someone always misses the announcements during service. The announcement should be done in such a way to create excitement. You want the entire church to feel this new endeavor will enhance the overall ministry of the church. Here is an example of an announcement which would be given by the pastor of the church:

"Many of you have come to these church services Sunday after Sunday, and have sung together during our times of praise and worship. You have enjoyed the singing so much that you may have wished or even prayed there would be a way in which you could sing more often. Well, today your prayers have been answered. We are officially starting a choir ministry here at the church. We already have the leadership in place to ensure its success. So if you feel called to this type of ministry, please come to an initial meeting (Day, Month) at (Time). I really feel that God desires to take us to another level in our praise and worship to Him, and we need your help to make it happen."

If you put an announcement in the church bulletin, or make a separate flier, make it exciting. You don't want the people who read it to think it's going to be a boring ministry. Allow at least a month of announcements before you have your first meeting. This will ensure that you have informed the majority of the congregation.

Step 2: The Auditions

This is the initial gathering of perspective choir members. I have found that most people are intimidated by the mention of an audition, no matter how talented they may be. You want to reassure everyone the audition is needed to find out where they are musically. Do whatever you can to ease the tension. One thing that works very well is a short time of praise and worship. This will help to get everyone in the right frame of mind and spirit.

After the people have gathered, and you have opened with prayer and praise, you are ready to begin.

The first order of business is to have everyone complete a choir member application. Here is an example of one I have developed:

CHOIR APPLICATION

Name:_____Date:_____

Address:_____ City:_____ Zip:_____

Home Phone: (   )_____ Work Phone: (   )_____

Birth Date:____/____/____ (You must be at least 18 years of age.)

Marital Status: Single_____ Married_____

Children: Yes_____ No_____ Ages_____

Are you currently a member of the church?_____ How long?_____

If not, how long have you been a regular attender here?_____

Are you presently enrolled in the membership class?_____

Please check one. Your answer does not automatically disqualify you from being a member of the choir.

YES   NO

_____ _____ 1. Have you received Jesus as Lord and Savior?

_____ _____ 2. Have you received the Baptism of the Holy Spirit?

_____ _____ 3. Have you kept yourself from using alcoholic beverages, tobacco products, or illegal drugs for the past 12 months?

_____ _____ 4. Have you kept yourself from immoral sexual activity such as fornication, adultery, incest, or homosexuality for the past 12 months?

_____ _____ 5. Have you needed any special counseling in the last 12 months?

What vocal part do you sing? Soprano____ Alto____ Tenor____ Bass___

What instrument, if any, do you play?_____ How long?_____

Briefly summarize your musical background? _____
_____

Why do you want to be a part of the music ministry?_____

There are many reasons for this type of application. First, it will help you in the audition process. You will want to make notes on the application regarding the applicant's singing ability. Answers to certain questions will give you an idea of the applicant's motives, and where they are spiritually. It will identify any major issues in their life that might hinder their ability to minister effectively. Yes, they could lie. But the truth has a way of manifesting itself.

Once everyone has completed the application, you are ready to audition them one at a time. I suggest you do this in a separate room if possible. This way the applicant is less distracted. The actual audition can be as simple or complicated as you want it to be, depending on what type of choir you are trying to assemble. If your choir members will be required to sight read, then your audition will need to include a sight reading test, in addition to hearing their tonal quality, vocal range, and ability to match tones. If you simply want choir members who can sing what they hear, and also harmonize, your audition process will be simpler.

Most of the choirs I have dealt with have not been required to have the ability to sight read, although we may at times teach that skill. Therefore, I usually have the choir applicant sing a simple praise song. This allows me the opportunity to hear everything I need in order to make a fair decision. I also make them harmonize with me, to make sure they can stay on their vocal part. You should be able to audition each applicant within five minutes. Don't be afraid to make suggestions to an applicant, or even have them sing something two or three times. You want to make sure you hear enough to make a fair decision. Remember to make

72

notes on the application, so when you review the applications later you don't have to try to remember what an applicant sounded like.

Don't feel obligated to tell an applicant right after their audition whether they passed. Tell them you will contact them as soon as a decision has been made. You want enough time to prayerfully consider every applicant. Once you have done this, you can invite those choir members who have successfully passed the audition to the first official choir rehearsal. Those applicants who did not pass also need to be contacted. Have a one-on-one meeting with them, and explain to them the reasons for your decision.

Step 3: The Rehearsals

Once you have assembled the people whom you feel will make up the choir, you are ready to start your initial rehearsals. It is at this time that you want to set forth your choir guidelines. This should include information regarding choir officers, rehearsal schedules, and choir uniforms. You also want to hand out any other useful materials that will help your choir members to be more effective in their ministry. Like, uhm...maybe a copy of this book? Some kind of choir packet works great, because it makes the choir member feel like they are a part of something special.

Included at the end of the choir guidelines I currently use, is a Statement of Agreement, which is a commitment each choir member makes to the Lord regarding their participation in the choir ministry. Here is an example:

CHOIR MINISTRY
STATEMENT OF AGREEMENT

Having read the requirements and procedures of the music department, I,_____, make a commitment of my person, time and talent to serve as a member of the choir ministry. In making this commitment I have resolved in my spirit that:

1. I am called by God and led by His Spirit to be involved in the music ministry of this church.

2. I will submit myself to the leadership, policies and procedures of the music department.

3. I am committed to the leadership, vision and work of this church.

4. I will attend all scheduled rehearsals and services to the best of my ability.

5. I will continually pray for the music department, its leadership and my fellow choir members.

_____   _____

Signature   Date

This commitment is between the choir member and God. Therefore, while we do ask them to sign it, we don't require them to return it to us. It is a reminder to them of their pledge and commitment to God to be faithful in the ministry to which they feel called.

During rehearsals you want to teach new music material. You also want to set a target date for the choir's debut. Make sure the entire church knows about this special day.

Step 4: The Choir Debut

All of the hard work, the auditions, the training, and the rehearsals were to musically and spiritually prepare the choir for this day. This is the official public beginning for your choir ministry. This is an exciting day! Here are some helpful suggestions to ensure this day is most effective.

1. Make sure you announce the target debut date during the first official rehearsal. This gives the choir something to work toward. It also gives them a chance to invite their family and friends.

2. You definitely want the choir to be in some type of uniform for their debut. So decide during the first few rehearsals what the choir's attire will be. (Remember, inward as well as outward.) Give the choir members plenty of time to get the uniform you decide on.

3. Have the pastor introduce the choir when it is time for them to sing. This reassures the congregation that the pastor is in full support of this new ministry.

4. Have a brief dedication ceremony, where the pastor publicly prays for the choir, and formally dedicates them into the service of the Lord.

5. Have a choir reception following the debut service to celebrate the occasion.

Once this day is over, you are on your way. Continue to do what you can to keep excitement in the choir. Try to have a new song to teach the choir at least every other rehearsal. Also, do whatever it takes to keep a spirit of unity in the choir. Choir fellowships and periodic outings work great. The collective effort a choir puts forth during the week to be both musically and spiritually prepared, will directly reflect on how effective their ministry is on Sundays.

---

*You may adapt the Announcement on page 70, the Choir Application on page 71, and the Choir Ministry Statement of Agreement on page 74 for use with your choir.

8

From My Heart to Every Part

In this chapter, I would like to share some final thoughts with the four major parts which make up the music ministry. My heart's desire is for the music ministry, for which you are called, to become all that God originally intended it to be.

The music ministry in any church is made up of four very important parts. They are:

1. The Pastor

2. The Music Director

3. The Singers (Choir Members)

4. The Musicians

Each of the above, individually or collectively, can make a vast difference in the overall effectiveness of a music ministry. If any of these parts fail to understand God's purpose for music in the temple, the ministry will probably experience mediocrity and spiritual defeat. Therefore, in this closing chapter, I have penned a personal letter from my heart to each part. I pray that God will speak to your heart as you read the letter that pertains to you, and that you will truly understand God's purpose for the music ministry in your church.

Reader:

    You have my permission to duplicate any of the
following letters as they are, or to write your own
letters, using these as your guide.

Alvin D. Fruga

Dear Pastor:

A writer once said, "The ideal role of the pastor in church music is one where the pastor provides leadership in service objectives, mutually arrives at overall goals or objectives for the music program with the minister of music, and functions in the role of counselor to the minister of music."[16]

The vision and purpose of the music program should be directly related to your corporate vision for the church. It is your responsibility to make sure this vision is adequately communicated to your music director as it relates to the music of the church. This will determine the direction the music program takes in terms of music styles, song selection, types of choirs and instruments.

Although you may not be a musician or singer, you need to be able to communicate to your minister of music the type of praise and worship and choir songs you prefer. This can be accomplished by simply giving the music director some examples on cassette. Music sets the tone and atmosphere in the services, and you must agree with the tone that's being set. Open communication between the minister of music and yourself is critical.

One of the most critical decisions you will ever make concerning your church is who you choose to be your minister of music. This person is usually in front of the congregation just as much as you are. Therefore, the person you select can be either a tremendous blessing to your church, or a spiritual detriment. Don't settle for anything less than God's standards for a minister of music. You should never appoint a music director who has a musical preference or style contrary to what you desire. You should always feel free to communicate your suggestions for certain songs. At the same time you should allow the music director a certain amount of freedom to express his or her ideas and gifts within the bounds of the corporate vision. "If a pastor is the right kind of pastor, he wants the minister of music to know how to meet the spiritual needs of people through music."[17]

Finally, I caution you not to make the same mistake King David make when he initially decided to bring the ark back to Jerusalem. After a disastrous attempt in 1 Chronicles 13, King David gives the main reason for his failure in 1 Chronicles 15:13:

> "...We did not inquire of him about how to do it in the prescribed way."

It is my prayer that you will consistently inquire of the Lord about how to usher His presence into your services, and that you will have a clear revelation as to the major role the music ministry plays in achieving this goal.

Dear Minister of Music:

God has not only called you, but He has also chosen you to plan and administer the entire music program of the church you attend. This of course includes the oversight of one or more choirs, the band, and perhaps a praise team. As minister of music, it is your responsibility to make sure the music program is going in the direction prescribed by you and the pastor of the church.

Always remember you work for and report to your pastor. The pastor is the final authority on the music of his church. He has the right to reject the use of a song, even if you don't agree with his reasoning. A pastor also has the right to suggest a certain song be taught to the choir or band. Maybe he heard it on the radio or television, or at a church he was visiting. The pastor may want to be informed of any new songs you are planning to teach to the choir and congregation. As the leader, he has that right, and it is essential that communication from him be welcomed by you at all times.

Encompassed in the many abilities of a leader is the ability to care and serve. You are not simply one who can teach songs, play an instrument, or conduct a choir. You are a servant. I have found that a great percentage of what I do as a minister of music has nothing to do with music at all. Singers and musicians have many of the same serious needs and concerns as people in the congregation. The most important thing you can do for them is to show genuine concern for their needs. This is the only way you can earn the privilege of being followed. Choir members don't want or need a dictator. The authority you have been given should never be abused. They need a leader with the attributes and characteristics of Christ. They don't need someone who will talk at them, but with them. Each member is looking for a sense of belonging and significance. They may never say it, but they want to know the small part they are contributing is not only special, but appreciated. And believe me, it is.

Finally, as a minister of music, you no doubt are very talented. You are most likely held in high esteem by your pastor, congregation, choir and band members, very similar to that of Lucifer. I encourage and also warn you in the name of the Lord, not to make the same mistakes Lucifer made. You can't live any kind of lifestyle and expect God to be pleased with your praise. Neither can you truly succeed on just the "outward adorning" of your gift. Your special talents and gifts are nothing without the anointing of God. And the anointing or approval of God is going to require much more of you than just a song and dance. It is going to require that you live a life yielded to the lordship of Christ on a daily basis.

It is my deepest prayer for you that you will not be thrown off track by the many compliments and accolades you will receive, and that you will remain humble, always realizing that every good and perfect gift comes from the Father above.

Your brother in Christ,

Dear Singers:

You are the special ones whom God has specifically chosen and set aside for the purpose of ministering unto Him in the Holy Place. God has given you as a gift to the pastor of your church. You don't just have the spirit of praise, you also possess the spirit of Levi. You have been given the awesome responsibility of singing forth the truth. You are spiritually going before your pastor with praises and shouts of deliverance in order to make the ground fertile for the Word he or she will deliver. But remember, you cannot sing forth the truth unless you are operating in truth with one another.

As choir members, you are an extension of the congregation, in that you were congregational members first before you became choir members. In that sense, the congregation easily relates to you, and will even tend to mimic you during church services. You must always be aware that you are an example. If the choir does not clap, the congregation probably will not clap. If you don't smile and look excited, the congregation probably will not respond to your ministry. Generally speaking, a dead choir produces a dead congregation, but a vibrant choir excites those in attendance. You must always sing with fervency, realizing that you are actually prophesying to God's people in song (1 Chronicles 25:1).

Your ability to sing does not automatically qualify you to become a choir member. And conversely, your inability to sing does not necessarily disqualify you from becoming a vital part of the music ministry. What matters is that you have a sincere desire to minister unto the Lord in song, and be willing to be trained in order to maximize your musical potential.

Many people join choirs for the wrong reasons. This causes major problems with both leadership and fellow choir members. The usual result is that there will be more than one vision, or division, in the choir. Some people join a choir because of its social value. Others join because they have a hidden agenda to get in the spotlight. However, the only reason one should become a part of the choir ministry is because they feel called to that particular ministry.

Finally, always remember that God chose you based on what He invested in you musically and your willingness to serve. Being a choir member is therefore a privilege, not a right. Don't take your ministry for granted. Make sure you are in your place at the prescribed time so that the service of the Lord can go as planned (2 Chronicles 35:15,16).

It is my sincere prayer that God will reward you for the countless hours you have given, and will continue to sacrifice for the sake of the ministry. I pray that He will multiply back to you all you've given in the ways you need it the most. I pray that you will have a renewed understanding regarding your ministry, and that He will anoint you afresh from this day forward.

In His service,

Dear Musicians:

The word *musician* is taken from the word *muse*, which means to consider thoughtfully, ponder or meditate.[18] As a musician, you are called to provide accompaniment for the singers. Your music sets the atmosphere or mood for which the words of a song will travel to the listener's heart. If the music is distracting, the message will not be effectively communicated. In many of the scriptures that we have already looked at regarding choirs, the musicians were right there with the singers. The scripture that really makes this point clear is 2 Chronicles 5:13,14:

> The trumpeters and singers joined in unison, as with one voice, to give praise and thanks to the Lord. Accompanied by trumpets, cymbals and other instruments, they raised their voices in praise to the Lord and sang: "He is good; his love endures forever." Then the temple of the Lord was filled with a cloud, and the priests could not perform their service because of the cloud, for the glory of the Lord filled the temple of God.

It is very clear that the deciding factor for the manifestation of God's glory was the fact that the musicians and singers were ministering as one. The musicians were not trying to drown out the choir. Nor were they too busy trying to play individual solos that they missed their cues. You must not consider yourselves separate from or superior to the choir. The two must work together in perfect unity, as one. Otherwise, you will never experience the true manifestation of God's glory.

Being a musician is a priestly office of ministry. In other words, you must be careful to live a godly life, because God will not settle for good musicians who live unclean lifestyles.

My prayer for you is that you will listen for the music and melodies of heaven rather than imitate the music of the world. Be open to God's musical will for your life. Spend time with Him, and allow Him to speak to the heartstrings of your soul.

Your fellow musician,

Summary Questions

Here are some of the major points we have discussed in this book. I strongly suggest that you periodically read these questions, and restudy some of the scripture references to constantly remind yourself of God's purpose for the music ministry. (Warning! If you have not read the entire book, you will not do very well on these questions.)

1. Who did God originally choose for the music ministry? Why?

2. What does the name *Levi* mean?

3. What are some of the steps God took to separate the Levites?

4. What were some of the duties of the Levites, and how were they paid?

5. Who in the Bible was most noted for their organization of the music ministry?

6. What do you remember the most about this person regarding his work in the music ministry?

7. Who were the three sons of Levi, and their most important musical descendants?

8. Who did the first choirs in the Bible sing to?

9. What is the Hebrew definition of the word *singers*?

10. What are the four basic translations of the word *singers*?

11. What are the requirements for ministering in the temple?

12. What is the most important thing a choir member can wear? Give a Scripture reference.

13. What are the three basic reasons why the music should sometimes stop?

14. How important is the choir ministry in the Church, and how does it compare to the praise team ministry?

15. What are the basic steps to organizing a choir?

Endnotes

1 James Strong, LL.D, S.T.D., *The New Strong's Exhaustive Concordance of the Bible* (Nashville, TN: Thomas Nelson Publishers, 1990), Dictionary of the Hebrew Bible, p. 47.

2 *Ibid.*, p. 59.

3 Strong, *Strong's Exhaustive Concordance*, Dictionary of the Hebrew Bible, p. 52.

4 *Ibid*, p. 89.

5 Funk & Wagnalls, *New International Dictionary of the English Language* (Newark, NJ:Publishers International Press, 1984), p. 234.

6 *Ibid.*, p. 111.

7 Strong, *Strong's Exhaustive Concordance*, pp. 114,115.

8 *Ibid.*, p. 114.

9 Strong, *Strong's Exhaustive Concordance*, Dictionary of the Greek Testament, p. 12.

10 *Ibid.*, p. 72.

11 Funk & Wagnalls, *New International Dictionary*, p. 1324.

12 Strong, *Strong's Exhaustive Concordance*, Dictionary of the Greek Testament, p. 9; and Funk & Wagnalls, *New International Dictionary*, p. 1348.

13 Herbert Lockyer, Sr., *Nelson's Illustrated Bible Dictionary*, (Nashville, TN: Thomas Nelson Publishers, 1986), p. 657.

14 Strong, *Strong's Exhaustive Concordance*, Dictionary of the Hebrew Bible, p. 33.

15 *Ibid.*, p. 89.

16 Robert Berglund, *A Philosophy of Church Music* (Chicago, IL: Moody Press, 1985), p. 83.

17 William L. Hooper, *Ministry & Musicians* (Nashville, TN: Broadman Press, 1986), p. 110.

18 Funk & Wagnalls, *New International Dictionary*, p. 837.

ABOUT THE AUTHOR
ALVIN D. FRUGA

Alvin D. Fruga — *Minister of the Word, Praise and Worship Leader, Soloist, Composer, Producer, Author* — there is no one word that adequately describes this man and his ministry. Alvin began his ministry at a very young age. From playing the piano and singing in church as a young boy, to working with groups and choirs in Southern California, he has always been heavily involved in the music ministry.

In 1980, Alvin's desire to continue to use his talents for the Lord led him to Oral Roberts University in Tulsa, Oklahoma. He served as Music Director for the "Souls A 'Fire" Ensemble, and was a member of the Oral Roberts Television Singers. He returned to California in 1983 to complete his formal education.

During the summer of 1986, Alvin graduated from college with a Bachelor of Science degree in Finance, Real Estate and Law, was ordained to the ministry, and married his childhood sweetheart, Sennola V. Fruga. In 1990, the Lord led Alvin and Sennola back to Tulsa where they submitted their gifts and talents to the leadership of Higher Dimensions Family Church, under the pastorate of Bishop Carlton D. Pearson.

Alvin became full-time Minister of Music for Higher Dimensions in 1992, and served faithfully in that capacity for four years. During this time, he served as

Praise and Worship Leader and Choir Director, not only for Higher Dimensions, but also for the Azusa Conferences held annually in Tulsa and other major cities across the country. He has traveled extensively with Bishop Pearson, ministering across the United States, Canada, the United Kingdom, Europe, and South Africa.

In addition, Alvin served as Musical Director, Song Writer, Arranger, Lead Vocalist, and Associate Producer for all of Bishop Pearson's major recording projects on the Warner Alliance label. The first project, entitled *Carlton Pearson and the Higher Dimensions Choir — Live*, was nominated for a Stellar Award and two Dove Awards. The song *"We Win,"* penned by Alvin for this project, was nominated for *"Song Of The Year."* The second release, entitled *Carlton Pearson — Live at Azusa*, exceeded the success of the first album in just a few months, and was nominated for *"Album of the Year."* Six of the eight songs on this project were written by Alvin.

Feeling led to further pursue God's call, Alvin and Sennola founded **FRESH OIL MINISTRIES** in April of 1995. With the support and blessing of Bishop Pearson, Alvin subsequently resigned his position as Minister of Music at Higher Dimensions in the fall of 1996. Alvin says, *"My heart's desire is to pour out on the world that which God has poured into me."*

Under the auspices of **FRESH OIL MINISTRIES**, and the spiritual covering of Higher Dimensions Family Church, Alvin preaches and teaches the Word of God, conducts Praise and Worship Seminars and Choir Clinics, and ministers special music for churches and conferences across the United States and world.

Alvin and Sennola, along with their four children — Michael, Teree, Kambri, and Shannon — currently reside in Tulsa, Oklahoma, and continue as members of Higher Dimensions Family Church. Alvin is undoubtedly on the cutting edge of every aspect of ministry. After all that has already transpired in and through this young man's yielded life, one can only imagine where God will take him and his ministry in the very near future. If you have never experienced the ministry of Alvin D. Fruga, you are undoubtedly in for a *"fresh"* surprise!

"But my horn shalt thou exalt like the horn of an unicorn: I shall be anointed with fresh oil"
(Psalm 92:10 KJV)

FRESH OIL MINISTRIES
P. O. Box 54542 • Tulsa, Oklahoma 74155

You are blessed to be holding what could become a collection piece, the first book ever written by Alvin Fruga. However, it will not be the last. For information on upcoming books, teaching tapes, and recording projects by Alvin Fruga, please write to the address below.

Alvin Fruga is available to minister in Word and song at your church, conference, or retreat. From leading praise and worship and ministering special music for conferences, to conducting music ministry seminars and teaching the Word, Alvin Fruga will infuse a fresh anointing in to any ministry function. For more information please contact:

Alvin D. Fruga

FRESH

OIL

MINISTRIES

P. O. Box 54542
Tulsa, OK 74155-0542